All Scripture references taken from the KJV of the Holy Bible, unless otherwise indicated.

DEEP POVERTY : get out of poverty & its shame by Dr. Marlene Miles

Freshwater Press 2025

Freshwaterpress9@gmail.com

ISBN: 978-1-967860-37-1

Paperback Version

Copyright 2025, Dr. Marlene Miles

All rights reserved. No part of this book may be reproduced, distributed, or transmitted by any means or in any means including photocopying, recording or other electronic or mechanical methods without prior written permission of the publisher except in the case of brief publications or critical reviews.

Table of Contents

Introduction 5

On A Tree 7

Redeemed 12

How the Tree Killed 20

Jesus Took the Tree 26

Lynch Bros 28

Evil Councils, Mobs and the Nature of Satan 31

Worse Than Being Shot 37

The Name 42

The Shame 47

Humiliation, Downgrading a Man's Humanity 58

Nakedness Has Strings 66

The Redeemer 72

The Tethering 77

The Devil & Trauma 80

Turned for Good 82

God Sends a Deliverer 93

Hating Your Deliverer 98
Coveting Honor 102
We Will Do It Our Way 106
Things that Tend to Poverty 113
It's Spiritual 117
Don't Reject Your Deliverer 121
Prayers 134
Dear Reader 135
Important Notes: 136
Prayerbooks by this author 137
Other books by this author 138

DEEP POVERTY

Introduction

The Holy Spirit gave me this title and also this book. I am describing Deep Poverty as poverty that has been in a person, family, bloodline, community, territory, city, state or nation for three or more generations. It's embedded and tenacious.

More than 37 million people in the US live in poverty. Nearly 700 million people live in poverty worldwide with more than 430 million living in Sub-Saharan Africa.

World Bank and other bureaus and organizations that gather this kind of data say that those who live in extreme poverty are existing on less than $2 per day.

However, this will not be a book of numbers, but a spiritual book to help us all understand and make spiritual impact against poverty in our own lives. In so doing, may we both share and teach others what is in this volume to set people free.

By Deep Poverty I mean collectively--, one or two people may be living as king of the hill, but if most of the people are impoverished and have been for generations, then there is deep and embedded poverty.

On A Tree

    Christ died to redeem mankind from poverty, sickness, death, and eternal damnation and He did it on a Tree: the Cross at Calvary. If poverty was fixable or correctable in the natural, Christ would not have had to die to make remedy for mankind. Man could have fixed it himself, for himself and as easily for others.

    Poverty is spiritual. If it were not, we could give the panhandler standing on the corner some money and all his financial issues would be corrected forever and never return--, say, the next day or even later that same day.

    The Salvation of the Lord is real. It is complete. It is redemption from sickness, poverty, and death. If Jesus came and died for mankind to be redeemed from poverty and we are not, then we must look deeply because **there is a deep problem.** If we are aware that we've been redeemed and we appropriate that redemption from poverty for ourselves, but there is still poverty, we should next check in the Courts of Heaven. Is there any entity or power violating the promises, laws, and ordinances of God?

No?

Then the person who is in poverty is the problem. Now, this book is not to judge anyone, it is to help you get out of poverty, lack, and insufficiency.

Some who are in poverty blame others. The may blame people they know and people they don't know. The job. The man. The government. The weather. Anything. But have we taken a good look at ourselves?

Yet so many want to correct the issue of poverty, even deep poverty, by legislation and natural remedies. Reparations? Well, if you owe someone or some people money, then you should pay them because owing debt is not of God. Owing debt leads to poverty, or more poverty, even deep poverty. Owing debt can be spiritual debt as well as debt in the natural.

Historically, those who are in political and spiritual power can invite poverty into a society and may be instrumental in it becoming spiritually embedded into the foundation of that society. The evil spiritual foundation is given permission by the evil political foundation. Vote, yes be sure to vote, but know this: political figures are put into position by spiritual powers and councils, unless they are opposed spiritually by God's people in prevailing and warfare prayers, and defeated.

Most often political actors go along with the get along because it becomes all about them, personally very soon once they are elected, or appointed. Else, why are so many people in power corrupt? Especially in political positions? Either they are easy to corrupt, or they are already corrupted when they get there.

A political player with no vision is the most dangerous. They are working only for today, do not see a big picture, do not believe there is a big picture, and they do not care. I'd venture to say that most are not spiritual. Some may pose for photo ops in formal churches. Those images may be of them sitting on a pew trying to stay awake. Or they could be standing in the pulpit speaking—talking about something that is not God and not spiritual. Usually, if they are speaking it is about something vague and innocuous, for the sound byte or photo op, as not to offend many people.

That sound bite is usually something generic. How then do we expect that generic, possibly religious, and often carnal someone to know anything about spiritual things? How do we expect them to know that poverty is spiritual? Or, to know how to fix it? Or to care? Or to know that deeply embedded poverty exists, how it got that way, and what to do to get rid of it?

Jesus said, *The poor you have with you always.* All-knowing Jesus knew that man would not figure this out or he wouldn't care, or that the entanglements that create and maintain poverty in a bloodline or society would be many, possibly complex, and subtle. So, mankind thinks that poverty, a spiritual condition, can be solved politically? This doesn't mean that there shouldn't be political cooperation and help, but if God sent Jesus to redeem us from poverty, and Jesus didn't take over the natural government, then poverty is solved spiritually.

A man who thinks that poverty can be solved socially? --, well, keep giving people money and see what happens if they are spiritually entangled by the *spirit of poverty* and the other spirits that work with it to tie a man up financially.

Jesus came to seek and save those that are lost. If a man is lost spiritually, and they are not accepting of the spiritual help that Jesus came to provide, then it should be no wonder that poverty will be that man's companion in life.

Redeemed

Redeemed means bought back. Bought back means something was lost or sold already. Redeemed—re-purchased.

What was sold?

Well folks, sin sells a soul out. When a man's soul is sold, poverty is a result. That means that a whole, well-ordered soul is how we stay out of poverty, God's way. It also means that the wealth of a man is contained by means of his soul. This doesn't mean that a man with a corrupt soul, or no soul at all can't have wealth. It usually means that he doesn't have it God's way, but will find a corrupt way that matches his corrupt soul or corrupts his soul in the way he may choose to get wealth, and that is usually by spiritual crime, or sin.

The blessings of the Lord maketh rich and
He adds no sorrow with it.

He restores my soul. (Psalm 23:5)

He restores my soul is part of the redemption, the re purchasing, re organizing and restoration of that man. Soul restoration is part of the Salvation of the Lord where a man's soul is taken off the trash heap and out of the salvage yard of the devil, where, if he has been sold, is being broken down for parts. He must be restored, rehabilitated in a sense--, not just his physical body, not just his good looks, not just his bank account, but his emotions, will, and intellect because out of it flow the issues of life. The issues are life and godliness; that is what man is put here for. To live his life and express his godliness.

We will come back to this, of course, but let's talk about how Christ has redeemed us.

Christ hath redeemed us from the curse of the law, being made a curse for us: for it is written, Cursed is every one that hangeth on a tree: (Galatians 3:13)

Cursed is everyone that hangs on a tree. Curses are spiritual. Spiritual means not only in the physical, but there is an unseen power or force working that is not seen or acknowledged by carnal folks.

Where did this hanging on the tree thing come from?

> And if a man have committed **a sin worthy of death,** and he be to be put to death, and thou hang him on a tree:

> His body shall not remain all night upon the tree, but thou shalt in any wise bury him that day; (for he that is hanged is accursed of God) that thy land be not defiled, which the Lord thy God giveth thee for an inheritance. (Deuteronomy 21:22-23)

Not only that, dead bodies are unclean in Jewish culture and they are usually buried the next day anyway.

The practice of hanging people from trees, often referred to in American history as lynching — has a long, brutal history that far predates the United States, but it has always been savage and brutal. Hanging on a tree, whether a real tree, or a gallows, took on particular racial and social significance in the 19th and early 20th centuries, in the USA.

In ancient times, hanging was used as a method of execution for centuries across many civilizations. In some cultures, trees were used when no gallows were available, however gallows may have been first used around 4,000 BC. This is saddening to think that man came out of a cave and said, *"Let's build a device to kill people on and let's make it as shameful as possible to disgrace the dead, the dying, and their families."*

The heart is deceitful above all things, and desperately wicked: who can know it?
(Jeremiah 17:9)

Public hangings were common in medieval and early modern Europe, often from trees or makeshift gallows.

In Colonial America, hanging was used as a legal form of execution for crimes. It was sometimes done from trees if no formal gallows existed. Executions were public spectacles, but not necessarily racially motivated in this early period. But it appears from time immemorial, that man exhibits a blood thirst that must be driven by the devil because God is not the author of this.

After the US Civil War, lynching became a terror tactic in the Southern United States, primarily targeting African Americans. From the late 1800s to mid-1900's thousands of Black men, women, and even children were lynched, often hanged from trees, by white mobs, many times without accusation, recourse, or trial.

These acts were meant to uphold the idea of white supremacy, suppress Black civil rights, and instill fear.

Trees were commonly used because they were readily available and symbolically tied to the lyncher having control over life and death — and over land.

A tree became a horrifying symbol of racial terror. In a society, anything can be weaponized and used as a threat against the disenfranchised and marginalized. We see historically that even something as natural and life-giving as a tree was twisted into a tool of death and domination. Additionally threats of calling the police on people or even dogs were also used to habitually threaten and torment Black people.

So, while hanging from trees has been used since ancient times and around the world, in the American context, it became a symbol of racist violence and social control during the Jim Crow era, especially from the 1870s to the 1950s.

People were hanged on trees or impaled on stakes as far back as Old Testament times. The Bible contains multiple references to execution by hanging from a tree, and it carries deep symbolic, judicial, and spiritual weight.

Deuteronomy 21:22–23 is the first Biblical mention and one of the earliest legal mentions of this type of death. Hanging a criminal's body on a tree was considered a public display of shame. The warning to bury them quickly shows reverence for the dead — even the condemned. Not being buried fittingly or at all is another whole curse.

> The eye that mocks a father, that scorns an aged mother, will be pecked out by the ravens of the valley, will be eaten by the vultures. (Proverbs 30:17)

Jezebel was eaten by dogs. All this connotes not being buried but left in the field to rot.

After defeating five Canaanite kings, Joshua "struck them down and killed them, and hanged them on five trees... but at evening they took them down. (Joshua 10:26-27). Hanging was used **after death**, not always as the method of execution. The tree was a **tool of public disgrace**, humiliation, and judgment.

In the book of Esther, Chapters 5–7, Haman built a gallows to hang Mordecai but ended up being hanged on it himself. Still, the concept of being "hung up" in view of others was meant as a warning and curse.

Absalom, David's rebellious son, is caught hanging by his hair in a tree, and then killed by Joab and his men. While not an official execution, the image of him suspended in a tree suggests divine judgment. (2 Samuel 18:9-15). Saints of God, whether a person is your parent or not, it would be wise to find out how much God loves them before attempting any evil against them. It seems Absalom didn't do that.

The New Testament connection to Jesus Christ is found in Galatians 3:13 (echoing Deuteronomy) *"Cursed is everyone who is hung on a tree."* This applies to Jesus' crucifixion.

Although Jesus died on a Roman cross, the Bible describes it symbolically as being "hanged on a tree" (Acts 5:30, 10:39, 13:29). This emphasizes that Jesus bore the Curse of sin and death in our place.

Being hanged on a tree was always connected to a curse, shame, judgment, or disgrace — whether the person died from the hanging itself or was displayed post-mortem.

And that same imagery carried forward into history, law, and later into racialized violence, turning something ancient into something too readily adapted by evil men and something deeply shameful and painful.

How the Tree Killed

Aside from the obvious asphyxiation by the noose, a tree was never designed to kill. The tree was created to glorify God and serve mankind. Employing a tree to kill a man is a reversal of authority. Those who used the tree for this evil imagination and heinous act are no different than those who use witchcraft. The tree is to serve man. The tree is not to kill man. Fruit and nuts on a tree are to nurture man, not bring death.

The fig tree that Jesus cursed in the New Testament was because there was nothing on the tree but leaves. Every tree should be useful and fruitful, and not just have leaves; leaves are for hiding as Adam showed us in Genesis. Not being fruitful is why Jesus cursed the fig tree. We might consider that a tree or any other of God's creation that is not doing what it is supposed to be doing could be a hindrance, an obstacle, a curse, or could be easily **diverted** for evil if it is not in it's purpose for being. The same is true of a man.

When a tree takes over a man, that man loses his dominion and authority; it is a curse to him. Dominion is a position in the hierarchy of God. It is God who gives us the power to get wealth. If we are no longer in position and authority, then that power has either been stolen or lost.

This could be how poverty comes as one of the results of being hanged on a tree.

Without the position, the authority, and the power to get wealth, a man cannot get wealth, and this begins the onset of lack, insufficiency, dearth and possibly poverty. When poverty gets fully embedded in the bloodline, I am calling that Deep Poverty. When a man or bloodline is in Deep Poverty no matter what they do, nothing seems to work--, or it works for a while. They work for a while, or they rise and fall, they gain and lose.

Emptiers, Swallowers, Devourers and Destroyers may be on the ready to take what that spiritually powerless man has gotten and usually he has gotten it by his own flesh with much toil and labor. So, he may have gotten it, either honestly or by hook and crook, but now he needs the **power** to keep it, especially if he is slated to remain in poverty.

> But thou shalt remember the Lord thy God: for it is he that giveth thee power to get wealth, that he may establish his covenant which he sware unto thy fathers, as it is this day. (Deuteronomy 8:18)

Saints of God, bookend your getting wealth in the Lord God. Wrap your prosperity in God so it will have power. Pray and declare on your way to work that it is God that gives you the power to get wealth. Then once you receive it remember the Lord God, for covenant, and also to keep, use and enjoy that wealth. **The power of wealth, the power that is in wealth will fight poverty** not just for the obvious natural reasons, but spiritually.

Does a man who is not acknowledging God in his finances know that he is <u>**spiritually powerless**</u> as it pertains to money and wealth? All his efforts will be by his flesh. He is denying himself a great power.

> Except the Lord build the house, they labour in vain that build it: except the Lord keep the city, the watchman waketh but in vain. (Psalm 127:1)

Except the LORD be in your getting money, you may be getting money in vain. Except the LORD build your bank account, are you building it in vain? I ask because that money has no spiritual power. The only thing that needs to happen is a spiritual attack against your wealth and without the LORD, that power could overpower you if the LORD is not your defense.

Does this man know if he is even spiritually alive or not? Most often he does not, so he may exert himself to exhaustion, spin wheels, try everything under the sun and never seem to either make ends meet, or get ahead. Until one day he may tire of that cycle and seek the Lord God.

By slated that he remain in poverty it could be written in **spiritual files** that this man, and or his bloodline should be impoverished or remain in poverty. How so? From judgments gotten in the Courts of Heaven by the Accuser of the Brethren who presents to accuse man night and day. Yes, the verdict is recorded.

Deep Poverty could be a result of not getting any wealth at all, or getting it and losing it by what may seem like chance, but it is either the Emptiers, Swallowers, Devourers or Destroyers. Against those and any other financial attacks, we need **power**.

We need power to get wealth, keep wealth, use wealth and enjoy wealth. Without power how do we fight off the forces that come to take it away? The man in Deep Poverty is often in slavery—spiritual slavery--, whether he knows it or not.

By the devices of the Serpent, a *tree* had already killed in the Garden of Eden, look at the beginning of poverty. Where everything was abundant, flourishing and very straightforward, a curse had to be issued and that curse was now:

And unto Adam he said, Because thou hast hearkened unto the voice of thy wife, and hast eaten of the tree, of which I commanded thee, saying, Thou shalt not eat of it: cursed *is* the ground for thy sake; in sorrow shalt thou eat *of* it all the days of thy life;

> Thorns also and thistles shall it bring forth to thee; and thou shalt eat the herb of the field;
>
> In the sweat of thy face shalt thou eat bread, till thou return unto the ground; for out of it wast thou taken: for dust thou *art*, and unto dust shalt thou return. (Genesis 3:17-19)

Instant, sudden, devastating. **Things just got hard. Adam, you have to get a real job now and it will take some effort because even the ground won't cooperate with you. Weeds, thorns, thistles will even trouble you, Adam, as, in your flesh you labor for food to eat.** This is poverty and it is because of a tree and disobedience and sin and a curse.

The Tree of the Knowledge of Good and Evil was the cause of death for Adam and Eve; they died spiritually when they disobeyed God and sinned, respectively.

There is a serious spiritual disruption and perversion when God's nature destroys man.

Jesus Took the Tree

Jesus took the *tree* for us. Historically, hanging on a tree started in the Ancient Near East. Hanging on a tree appears in Old Testament texts as early as Deuteronomy (ca. 1400–1200 BC). It was also practiced in Assyrian, Babylonian, and Persian cultures.

Hanging from a tree (or impaling on a stake/tree) was a form of execution or public disgrace, often used after death to shame the body. Five Canaanite kings were hanged on trees after being executed. They were already dead, so the shame of being left out on a tree was grievous in Bible times. The Romans didn't invent death by hanging, but they perfected it and made it a widespread tool of terror, especially from the 1st century BC through the 4th century AD. Crucifixion was used primarily for slaves, rebels, and non-Romans.

Jesus Christ who was all man and all God was crucified around 30–33 AD, fulfilling the Old Testament notion of "cursed is everyone who hangs on a tree" (Galatians 3:13). It is no accident that along with the help of Judas Iscariot the Pharisees and Sadducees tried to paint Jesus as a slave by paying Judas 30 pieces of silver to betray Jesus. Thirty pieces of silver was the going rate for a slave during that time.

Hanging on a tree predates crucifixion by at least 800–900 years.

It's not an accident that the Bible uses the phrase "hung on a tree" when referring to crucifixion, making the Cross a tree of death, but in Christ, it was transformed into a tree of life, fulfilling both ancient prophecy and spiritual redemption.

But hanging on a tree invoked the Curse of the Law, which includes poverty.

Lynch Bros

The term "lynch law" is generally traced back to Charles Lynch, a Virginia planter, magistrate, and Revolutionary War-era politician who lived near Lynchburg, VA.

During the American Revolution (1770s), Charles Lynch led illegal punishments against people suspected of being British loyalists. He and his neighbors formed a local council to judge and punish people without formal trial. They would whip, and jail those they accused, and they would also seize their property.

These actions were seen by some as patriotic, but they bypassed legal due process. This informal justice became known as "Lynch's Law" or "lynch law." While Charles Lynch didn't necessarily hang people from trees, the idea of vigilante-style punishment, or mob "justice" became attached to his name. (Lynchburg is named after his brother who was not a lyncher.)

By the 1800s, especially post-Civil War, the term "lynching" came to mean mob executions, especially hangings. These events were often racially motivated and evolved or devolved into racial terror.

Lynchings were public acts of terror that were used to enforce white supremacy. They were horrifying but often photographed and celebrated by participants. Folks get bold and brazen when they get away with stuff even once.

> Woe unto them that seek deep to hide their counsel from the LORD, and their works are in the dark, and they say, Who seeth us? and who knoweth us? (Isaiah 29:15)

By the next war on US soil, the American Civil War, hanging had evolved into racialized terror, especially against Blacks.

Blacks were not the only people lynched and sadly, if many had their way it might still be happening. From *Politico*, (5/25/22) **Betsy Woodruff Swan and Kyle Cheney** wrote: "We learn that the January 6, 2021 crowd at the US Capitol either was or had morphed into a would-be lynch mob. The Jan. 6 Select Committee has heard testimony indicating that then-President Donald Trump, after rioters who swarmed the Capitol began chanting "hang Mike Pence". These rioters expressed support for hanging Trump's then vice president, according to three people familiar with the matter."

Pence was neither Jesus, British, nor African American, so we must ask, who would inspire and still inspired such an act in our times?

The devil. The same devil, working through people.

In the US Colonies and United States, hanging started as vigilante justice. It turned into a national symbol of racial terror. And its roots — just like those trees — run deep and bitter. Historically, hanging on a tree came well ahead of Jesus' crucifixion, by many centuries but it still carries the curse and the terror. But no one in the entire world can pretend they don't know how brutal, savage, evil and shameful it is.

Evil Councils, Mobs and the Nature of Satan

What began in the Bible as a visible mark of judgment and curse was later weaponized in history by people trying to assign that same divine disgrace to others, especially Black bodies in America, implying that *anyone hung on a tree is under God's curse.*

Mobs who hung people weren't just killing, they believed they were making a theological statement, whether consciously or not: *"This one is cursed."* They were behaving as if they were God. If impersonating a police officer is a crime, what is the punishment for impersonating God, misrepresenting God's Word and authority?

It is difficult for me to think that members of a lynch mob or the KKK are Bible scholars to even know about Deuteronomy 21:23, so I suppose they were drawing on the older Persian and European history of brutal murder by hanging, evoking humiliation and shame. But perhaps they did know the Bible; stranger things have probably happened.

Here's the truth the enemy never counted on: Jesus took that Curse. He was hung on a tree for mankind, not because He was guilty, but so we could go free. The Tree? What others meant as a sign of shame, God used for redemption.

So, when people hang another person from a tree, pretending its justice or divine order, they're perverting a symbol that **God has already redeemed** through Christ.

Lynch mobs are evil councils in the natural, and or are a result of spiritual evil councils that meet to plan, condemn, thwart and destroy mankind. Evil councils form their own judgments through mock trials or no trials at all.

A person could be accused in a coven or other evil council, for example, and that person is spiritually unaware. He may be at home watching TV or sleeping having ignored the spiritual signs that he is now nominated as a candidate for evil or he is on an evil altar.

This is not the same as when the Accuser of the Brethren is at the Throne of God accusing man day and night and hoping to get a judgment against that man from God. That verdict is legal; it is from God. That man, though could still be unaware, at home watching TV, at a ballgame, or just goofing off somewhere not knowing that he has been called into the Courts of Heaven and a case is pending or being heard against him there.

Mobs who react on the judgments of evil councils do so with reckless abandon, because they believe they have moral majority, spiritual authority, or a mandate to do so. They may prevail, especially if the victim hasn't answered, hasn't called for Mercy, hasn't admitted to the sin, hasn't pleaded the Blood of Jesus, hasn't defended himself, and may not even be in Christ.

Both in Scripture and history, when there is a gathering of corrupt authorities such as kings, rulers, mobs, or religious leaders who are issuing judgments that God Himself never sanctioned, the innocent may be destroyed. The Sanhedrin (Jewish council) met to discredit and destroy Jesus. Were it not in the plan of God, it would have been impossible against Jesus, but not against a mere man who does not profess Christ or a dry Christian who doesn't pray.

> Now the chief priests and the whole council were seeking false testimony against Jesus to put him to death.
> (Matthew 26:59-66)

They *knew* He was innocent. They *twisted* law to justify a predetermined outcome. This was a spiritual and political lynching, with Rome carrying out the death sentence by hanging Him "on a tree" (the Cross).

In *1 Kings 21,* Jezebel assembled a false council and arranged for two false witnesses to accuse Naboth, so she could steal his vineyard for Ahab. Naboth was stoned to death based on a rigged judgment. An evil ruler used council corruption to carry out murder under the guise of legal justice. Jezebel is the *spirit* of a witch.

Shall the throne of iniquity, which devises evil by law, have fellowship with You?
(Psalm 94:20)

Some translations say: *"...which frames mischief by statute"* which neans, *legislated wickedness*. It's talking about governments or councils that make evil *look* legal.

In American history lynchings of Black people wasn't random. It was often organized, permitted, or ignored by **local councils**, sheriffs, courts, and churches. Law enforcement would do nothing about it. Judges would refuse to convict. Mobs became *de facto* evil councils, issuing extrajudicial, illegal, vigilante mob death sentences. Even local pastors sometimes remained silent or complicit.

These were false councils, wicked thrones, issuing ungodly judgments.

With 12% of the population of the USA living in poverty, we see nearly 20% of Blacks are impoverished. Was the curse of man by hanging on a tree and the social stigmata afterward instrumental in keeping certain people groups in poverty? Hispanics in the USA are only 14% impoverished, *fyi*.

> Woe to those who call evil good, and good evil. (Isaiah 5:20)

What wicked councils call "justice," Heaven calls murder. What man says is "deserved," God says is innocent blood crying out from the ground (Genesis 4:10).

What was meant to curse and destroy, God has already judged, and Jesus has already died to redeem us from it and its effects. **Systemic injustice** is judgement by evil councils either in the natural and in spiritual realms. An evil mob will send a man to the tree when he may not even be guilty of death, or guilty at all.

They did it to the prophets. They did it to Christ. They did it to the oppressed. But Jesus came to set the oppressed free. So, in Christ we can be free of all oppression, including poverty.

Worse Than Being Shot

That aforementioned meeting may have been orderly or it could, in the natural , have been a raving mob. Was there not a mob at the "trial" of Jesus? Were they not shouting to release Barabbas rather than Jesus? Mob mentality runs amok and takes on the nature of chaos.

As mankind took on the nature of Satan, they also weaponized trees against mankind. It is very witch-like to weaponize nature against humans. Witches will weaponize anything to their own desired, evil ends. Do they realize that is what they are doing? Some do. Many do. Some do not have a clue. They are blind witches.

The one who mutters that they hope some "natural disaster befalls another could either be a real witch or a blind witch. Depends on their own intent, awareness, history, and level of evil.

In the wild, wild, American West, hanging was the standard legal punishment and execution for capital crimes such as murder, horse theft, or robbery. The tree--, well the parts of a tree were already weaponized when gallows, often built near courthouses or jails, were used for formal, judicial, and public executions.

This was inherited from English common law, where public hanging was the norm. As we've seen in many western movies, it was the spectacle. People came for the shock and awe, if not, for macabre entertainment. Hanging was not always seen as heinous, it was considered routine justice. Especially on the western American frontier, lawmen, settlers, and vigilantes didn't always have courts, jails, or time for a proper trial. Bullets were expensive and better saved for defense or hunting. Rope and a tree were cheap, effective, and reuseable.

Makeshift justice was fast, and hanging didn't require reloading, as if a firing squad was humane or justified punishment for stealing a horse or looking at a white woman.

But, as said, man will take on the nature of whoever he is serving. The first example of a tree being weaponized against mankind was in the Garden of Eden and that was done by the Serpent.

Mob "Justice" and fear tactics will evolve wherever there is anarchy, lawlessness, or man has fully taken on the nature of the devil and declared himself the law, king, or a *god.*

"Neck-tie parties" were meant to send a message: *Cross the line, and you die*. Public hangings drew crowds and were intended to intimidate or control. In these cases, it could become especially heinous, violent, unfair, and racially or politically motivated.

When a vigilante party decided to use their own kind of justice they'd come up with whatever they thought was the absolute worst thing for their victim. Hanging had a long cultural association with shame, dishonor, and finality. To be hanged was often seen as worse than being shot, especially in honor-based cultures.

Shooting could imply a fair fight. Hanging meant you were *caught, judged, and dealt with*, and most often, publicly.

By tradition, colonial settlers deemed it to be legal because it was carried over from English law; it was official punishment. Mob justice must have given the community a sense of gatekeeping; they felt safe now, although their sense of peace may have only been a (temporary) lifting of oppression because they were appeasing the devil by shedding blood. Aside from making themselves feel safe or powerful they could have enjoyed a break from oppression from the *god* or devil they served because they had given that devil a sacrifice; they had given that devil blood. Satan is especially empowered when blood is shed, and no one even does anything about it because they've all decided to agree.

That ancient shadow of *"Cursed is anyone hanged on a tree"* still looms. Even in the dusty American frontier, the symbolism of the tree still whispered through the rope.

When people think they're just doing what's "practical" or "normal," they're often acting out spiritual patterns older than they realize. When people lead or follow a mob to carry out vigilante justice, they may only be doing what is deeply programmed within themselves while thinking they are doing something honorable, just, patriotic, or even spiritual.

Hanging someone from a tree, in the Wild West, whether it was quick justice, or brutal control, it was murder. In American history, it became a tool of racial terror. In the Bible, it's a symbol of curse and disgrace.

They "hanged" Jesus from that Cross at Calvary even as Jesus said, Forgive them for they know not what they do. Without clarity and discernment what man will understand the spiritual ramifications and fallout of what he does at any time?

Beneath it all, the entire world must know that it echoes something ancient and evil.

The Name

In some cultures, this curse and disgrace would now mean that the hung person's family would suffer because of being related to that person. The accused was already dead, so how could he (or she) suffer anymore on this side? The hanging was corporal punishment, but it was so much more; the Marshall or the mob was not only trying to curse a man to hell, but they were also sending out control signals to the community and the family as well as disgracing his family and bloodline.

If a person was hanged as cursed, did that curse fall on their family? Well yes, the person was already dead, but the disgrace of it would *live on*. This should tell you two things, that tree or gallows became an altar, because blood was shed there, and also this is spiritual, else the memory and shame of it would not live on. What is placed on an altar continues and lives on until a greater power stops it.

A public lynching is the hateful social media post of today. And, *is the Internet an altar?* Does the internet forget anything? Think of cyberspace where things are written and recalled at will. In the spirit when something is written, it can only be undone by a greater spiritual act.

In Biblical and ancient Middle Eastern culture, honor and shame were family-specific and collective, not just personal. A person's curse or disgrace affected their entire household, often for generations. If you were the son or daughter of a hanged man, people didn't just see your father as cursed — they saw you that way too. This is why lineage, bloodlines, and blessings mattered so much. Then, especially and even now sometimes, your family reputation could elevate or crush your destiny.

This is why God was so precise in cleansing bloodlines, redeeming names, and even **changing** names (Jacob to Israel, Abram to Abraham. It's why a guy named Jabez ask God to change his name--, and although that was his first name, the last name or surname of a family is important.

He that hath an ear, let him hear what the Spirit saith unto the churches; To him that overcometh will I give to eat of the hidden manna, and will give him a white stone, and in the stone a new name written, which no man knoweth saving he that receiveth it. (Revelations 2:17)

In compiling a dossier or creating a record (rap sheet) on someone, what is all that information attached to? The person's name. in the case of spiritual matters, it is attached to the bloodline name.

Written: let it be written this man is:… when poverty is **written** on a bloodline, that poverty is deep and there is family fallout.

This is what the Lord says:
"Record this man as if childless,
a man who will not prosper in his

lifetime,
for none of his offspring will prosper,
(Jeremiah 22:30A)

Visiting the iniquity of the fathers on the children to the third and fourth generation. Deuteronomy 5:9

When God looks on anyone, (in His "visits") He sees their bloodline as well as the individual. That's not saying God *delights* in punishing folks, but instead, it describes a spiritual and societal reality. Sin, shame, and curse had cascading consequences.

Achan's sin (Joshua 7:24-25) was the cause of his entire family being judged along with him. They all were stoned to death, then burned with fire. This wasn't just guilt by association, this was guilt and shame by blood. Achan stole from the spoils of war— were Achan's wife and kids fighting the battle? No, they were probably back home in the tent worried about their husband and father's safe return. Yet they also suffered in his evil choice to steal devoted things. The sin had spiritual roots that needed uprooting.

The entire family felt and bore the weight of inherited judgment, iniquity and also the disgrace. They died with the culprit. However, when entire families and bloodlines are not lost with the criminal perpetrator, they may for generations feel the weight of the iniquity of the sin of their relative.

> Our ancestors sinned and are no more, and we bear their punishment. (Lamentations 5:7)

When a man is in Christ however, he becomes a new man, and he gets a new name, Christian. That new name does not have shame, sickness, death or poverty written with it. Shall we then appropriate that for our life and godliness? The old dossier should pass away, the old file should be destroyed, but we must declare it and insist on it.

.

The Shame

The Salvation of the Lord allows us to escape from the Curse, iniquity and shame, but we must be **all in** Christ, not somewhere on the edge or on the perimeter of Christianity. And we must declare that we are in Christ and demand our rights in prayer, such as in the Courts of Heaven and walk uprightly before the Lord. That means being fully delivered, and resisting the devil so that he flees

That means **not** doing the things that are demonic snares and traps. But the subtlety of the devil is that man often doesn't see a trap as a trap. Instead, he sees things as his *right*. He believes that he has a right to be angry. He believes he has a right to be bitter. He believes it is his right to be greedy or, prideful. He thinks that it he decides not to forgive, then he is somehow powerful. All these works of the flesh are the **ropes** that tie that flesh to the Curse and we know within that Curse is poverty. These flesh acts are the ropes that hoist a man to a tree of shame; and poverty is a shame. Deep Poverty is a crying shame. But do we know if a man is acting out because he is frustrated and impoverished, or did acting out **cause** the poverty? What we do know is that acting out in the flesh will keep poverty in a person's life.

Traps?

Men believe it is their duty or right to chase women, fornicate, and commit all other kinds of sexual sins. They are convinced by the world that that is *living*.

These are traps. This is dying.

Some of the things that can tether a man to poverty or even Deep Poverty are blatant and obvious. Some are insidious, subtle and downright sneaky and hidden. Many sins are celebrated by the world, and the spiritual consequences of those sins are never mentioned.

Too many think that if no one gets pregnant, then illegal sex is free sex. Some think if they don't get an STD or STI, then they got off free. Not so. Each sin and its resultant iniquity are spiritual **ropes** that tie man to a tree—a tree of shame and curses.

Shame and humiliation have been used as a form of social control, forever. Shame isn't the same as guilt. Guilt says: *"I did something wrong."* Shame says: *"I **am** something wrong."*

Shame doesn't just touch what a man did, it attacks who he is, who he knows himself to be. Shame is weaponized to make a man believe who is who his evil neighbor tells him that he is, and nothing ore, and nothing better. It becomes a mark on his identity, not just a stain on his record.

The morning after escape from wherever a person fornicated is not called a ***walk of shame*** for nothing.

Shame silences a man. He stops speaking up. He won't ask for help, won't confess, won't lead. He fears being found out, even if the shame isn't his fault. A shamed man wears a mask and loses his voice. He may masquerade or try to assimilate to become something inauthentic, something different than himself.

That in itself is also spiritually disempowering and fatal.

Jesus bore the shame, the chastisement of our peace was upon Him. But read this verse very well:

> He was oppressed, and he was afflicted, yet he opened not his mouth: he is brought as a lamb to the slaughter, and as a sheep before her shearers is dumb, so he openeth not his mouth. (Isaiah 53:7)

Jesus did not speak. He opened not His mouth. Yes, it was in the plan of God, but shame will take a man's voice. He bore the shame of the sin of the world.

Shame paralyzes a man's purpose and makes him doubt his calling. He second-guesses every decision. "Am I good enough? Do I deserve this?" He may avoid responsibility, not because he's lazy, but because he feels unworthy.

Shame makes a man forfeit his assignment before he even begins.

Whoever is trying to use shame against another to take that man down a few notches, may take that man all the way down, leaving him notch less altogether. It could be full soul murder, leaving him in a pit.

Shame warps a man's identity. A man wrapped in shame will confuse failure with finality. He'll wear his mistakes like a name tag: He becomes defined by the thing he can't undo. *"I'm the one who messed up... got locked up... got her pregnant... got fired... didn't protect them..."*

Shame breeds anger or withdrawal. It can make a man explode defensively, using control or abuse. It could cause him to implode into depression, isolation, and addiction. Either way, he is thrust into survival mode — not thriving, not building, just hiding or fighting and trying to exist, to keep his head above water.

Adam covered himself with fig leaves and hid from God.

That's what shame still does. How many have deleted there entire profiles and pages after being exposed or shamed online?

Shame destroys relationships. A man in shame won't let people get close, even those who love him. He'll either push them away or cling to toxic validation such as sex, money, control, and ego.

He becomes unavailable, even if he's physically present.

Shame has a voice that continuously speaks. Shame *Lies*. *Shame says things such as:*

- "You'll never be clean."
- "Real men don't cry, talk, or ask for help."
- "You're too far gone."
- "You have to pay for this forever."
- "God's done with you."

These are lies straight from hell, designed to keep a man in chains, even when the prison door is open.

Every one of these behaviors resulting from shame is a tether to poverty. It is a tether to sickness and death. These are the ropes and ties that keep that man dangling in the tree that Jesus came and died for us to be out of. But as long as we, in our mind, soul, or spirit feel that we are still on the tree, then are we still on the tree? Or are we out of it today and back in it tomorrow with the next round of shame, or the next round of sin and its resultant iniquity.

This is how Deep Poverty gets a foothold and this is how it persists.

To be free from it, there must be a spiritual change and a renewing of the mind.

> He was despised and rejected... a man of sorrows, acquainted with grief. (Isaiah 53:3)

> Who for the joy set before Him endured the cross, despising the shame, and is now seated at the right hand of God. (Hebrews 12:2)

God doesn't just offer forgiveness; He offers **soul restoration**. He removes the disgrace from your name and bloodline. He will restore you to your right position of glory and honor and authority and dominion, but it is not by magic; you have to work so Deep Poverty does not persist.

As anyone feels the guilt and bears the iniquity of sin, God will blot that sin out with the Blood of Jesus. He will restore your voice, your vision, and your personhood.

To overcome shame a man needs:

- The Truth of God's Word, to rewrite the lies.
- A safe place to speak, where he can be real without being re-condemned.
- The presence of God. Shame cannot coexist with active Grace.
- Covenant community, not just friends, but people who won't leave when the mask falls off.

Shame tries to shrink a man and erase him—, to cut him off from the life of God. But Grace rewrites him. Grace says: *"You're still My son. Get up; you're not done yet."*

Shame wants a man silent, small, and self-hating. But God says:

> Instead of your shame, you shall have a double portion. (Isaiah 61:7)

Jesus came that we may have life and have it more abundantly. He fully redeemed mankind, else, He would not have said, "**It is done**," when it was all done. God cannot lie.

Every work of the flesh and its iniquity, ties a man back up on that tree when there is a greater Tree that has served as an altar to cleanse us and renew a right spirit in each of us who will accept. After that we must prosper our souls--, ourselves. Then the hard work of looking objectively at ourselves and asking why do we do the things we do? Why do we keep repeating family patterns? Grandma did it this way--, how did that work out for Grandma?

We must do the work to become new creatures in Christ, else we will repeat the same cycles, the same errors, the same sins and be caught up in the same strongholds just handing the devil rope to suspend progress and breakthroughs by tying folks up. This most often has to be spiritual work, because like-father-like-son--, like-mother-like-daughter is spiritual. It is genetic and spiritually genetic—we inherited it. Without spiritual work, little or nothing will change.

Work 14 jobs if you like. Go to school 20 years, if you are book smart, but without Christ you will still have the same results that is written of you in the spirit, unless you've done the spiritual work to blot it out and change it. These strongholds are what tether a man to that book and those evil ordinances--, try as he may.

> When you follow the desires of your sinful nature, the results are very clear: sexual immorality, impurity, lustful pleasures, idolatry, sorcery, hostility, quarreling, jealousy, outbursts of anger, selfish ambition, dissension, division, envy, drunkenness, wild parties, and other sins like these. Let me tell you again, as I have before, that anyone living that sort of life will not inherit the Kingdom of God.
> (Galatians 5:19-21)

The mind needs to be renewed. But all the ropes and ties and possibly chains that hold a person inside the pit of poverty or the deep pit of Deep Poverty may not be ropes of his own making. There could be so many ancestral ropes that it may seem overwhelming--, yeah, that's what gets people into Deep Poverty. The strongholds could be so many, so intricate, so tight, with types of knots you've never seen before, that even if he wants to do better or do *differently*, he can't because of his blood. What is in his blood, he is programmed to walk out unless he gets major spiritual help; that man needs deep deliverance in Christ to escape Deep Poverty.

Humiliation, Downgrading a Man's Humanity

In olden days, the stockade, or pillory was a wooden or iron frame with holes for the head and hands, or sometimes feet. The person was locked in place in a public area--, often a town square. Nowadays that public area is online in social media accounts. There's your avatar or image looking like something sticking through the circle of the stockade or through a yoke.

Usually, a person sent to the stocks was left there for a few hours to a couple of days, whatever was sufficient to humiliate and embarrass that person. They were not left there indefinitely. It was not their prison, but they were left there long enough for sunburn or worse, sunstroke or heatstroke. Insect bites, dehydration, heat exhaustion. Being mocked or spit upon or having rotten food thrown at them. They weren't put there or left there until death, but just long enough. The real damage wasn't always physical — it was social and reputational. There It was for public humiliation to expose sin or wrong behavior before the community

The goal was **shame, not just correction**. It was to let the whole town see what you've done, and never forget it. It was to make an example of someone, so others won't follow their path. It was to make a person never forget what they had done and make them never want to do it again, as in behavior modification. It was to bring a man to shame.

Why shame? Shame is a powerful tool and a tactic of the devil. Adam and Eve were ashamed after they realized they were naked. Whether stripped or not, feeling exposed leads to shame. Along with shame came the Curse of the Law – shame can affect your money. Shame will keep you at home instead of out there working and in the marketplace, where you can earn a living.

Sadly, as cruel as being publicly placed in stockades was, it worked--, not because of physical pain, but because of the **social fallout** which may have brought emotional pain.

Wait a minute!-- isn't that how some people have weaponized social media in our times? Maybe social media didn't start that way and maybe that was never the intention. But the heart of man is wicked.

A tree was never designed to kill a man, but the heart of man is wicked.

The stockades were evil under the guise of moral theater. In Puritan and colonial times, they didn't have TV, so punishment was a public event that people came out to see for either morbid curiosity or entertainment, although it was hyped as a method to reinforce moral values. Who, with moral values, would come out to watch such a thing?

The accused has no covering, no dignity, no protection. They are stripped of their standing in the community and reduced to their crime — publicly. The devil puts mistakes on blast.

But God, who is Love, covers a multitude of sins.

Add to that another method of public punishments: burning at the stake. Whether guilty or not, whether a real witch or not, don't you think that affected the accused witch's family even after she or he were burned alive? This is spiritually significant because humiliation, especially public humiliation, has always been a tool of judgment in Scripture and in society.

In the Bible, humiliation is often paired with:

- Sin exposure (Numbers 32:23) Your sin will find you out.
- Mockery of the innocent (Jesus was stripped, spat on, crowned with thorns. (Matthew 27:28–30).
- The breaking of pride—taking the haughty down a few notches. (Nebuchadnezzar in Daniel 4)

God draws a line; He doesn't take shame to a level of soul murder. Deuteronomy 25:3 says that when someone is beaten for a crime,

"...your brother should not be degraded in your eyes." That means: Even when someone is guilty, you don't get to erase their humanity.

Yet the devil has weaponized everything that he can--, even social media. The *pillory* of the past still lives on and echoes in our modern era.

- Online shaming and "cancel culture"
- Mugshots plastered on news and social media
- Humiliation used to control people long after the penalty is served

Sometimes, the humiliation outlasts the sentence.

Other acts used to inflict pain:
- Rape
- Other acts of physical assault
- Revenge porn

Revenge porn. (also called non-consensual intimate imagery) is the sharing of explicit images or videos of someone without their consent, often by a former partner, with the intent to humiliate, punish, or control. When a person sends such an image, she or he is building a **stockade** to put themselves into but trusting the other person won't betray them—like ever. (Better think first.) If the person using revenge porn against another for their destruction, their image, job, career, and relationships– it's as though they've built a gallows to hang their victim on.

Sending sexy pix is a lot of power to put in the hands of someone that you want to have sex with; however, sex is more powerful than people may want to realize.

Sexting is one of the modern digital equivalents of the stockade — but sexualized, public, and devastating. And as we've been discussing, it's not just physical or legal, it's deeply spiritual and psychological warfare.

It is so vicious because it weaponizes intimacy, and most often in a sneak or shock attack. What was once private, even legal, between married couples can turn into a weapon to be used as a tool of punishment.

Revenge porn is about power and domination. The goal is not just exposure but degradation. It mirrors ancient shame tactics:

"You will be stripped, displayed, and unable to cover yourself."

However, the protections in God are limited until you repent because porn images belong to the devil, not the person you sexted them to and not to you whose image it is. Further, the owner of the social media platform now has legal ownership of whatever you post--, even sexy pix. These nudes and sexy images are inspired and spawned by the devil, and they belong to the devil. These are the types of images kept in a spiritual file against a person.

No, I'm not trying to shame anyone more by saying that. I am trying to warn all the people who have not ready sent out images that can be used as weapons against them later on--, don't do it.

Revenge porn causes ongoing trauma. Victims often suffer anxiety, depression, social isolation, and even suicidal thoughts. The internet doesn't forget, therefore the digital footprint can **linger forever**, even if legally removed.

What is most damning about the act is the living victim's response to what has happened to him or her. This is the trap. Shame is a trap. Now the person has a flesh or carnal response to the shame that ties him to the Curse and for the intents and purposes of this book – he is tied **more** to poverty than he was before, so the problem intensifies.

Social media can be made into an evil altar. Worse than that is the sexted images can be easily screenshot or downloaded and placed on an evil altar and in a coven or other satanic circle, worse can be done to a person by their pictorial representation, especially a nude image. Those who are especially evil may curse certain body parts to not work for the victim again, properly, or *ever*.

No weapon formed? Then stop making weapons against yourself. Let your moderation show. Do all things decently and in order. Maintain your dignity and honor. Keep your spiritual and natural garments on and maintain the glory that God placed on you.

Nakedness Has Strings

If we are warned in the Bible not to look on the nakedness of others, then why would we send nakedness to someone? Wouldn't that be placing a stone of offence in front of a person? Entrapment? As well as compromising yourself if not today, in the future? We are not supposed to spy out the liberties of others--, that is look at what they are working with.

Noah's son Ham, exposed his father's nakedness instead of covering him (Genesis 9:22–23). God cursed Ham's lineage for it. *Why?* Because the intent was to mock and dishonor, not to restore or protect.

- Reuben lay with his father's concubines in a public way.
- Abasalom laid with his father's concubines in view of all of Israel.

The woman caught in adultery in John 8 was dragged out, exposed in public, surrounded by a **mob** ready to stone her. But Jesus shifts the spotlight onto the accusers, and He covers her with Mercy, saying: *"Neither do I condemn you. Go and sin no more."*

Even if your sin has found you out, especially sexual sin, plead Mercy.

In some states and many countries revenge porn is still legal, but most now have laws criminalizing the distribution of non-consensual explicit material with the intent to harm, harass, or embarrass another. The emotional and spiritual damage often goes far beyond legal recourse.

Revenge porn is like virtual rape—it could be called visual rape, and it is intended to shame the victim in the image. However, everyone who views the images also becomes a victim whether they realize it or not. Looking on porn initiates you into darkness. When a person views the nakedness of another, spiritually, they have married that person. Viewing the sex act of others: you have married them—both (or all) of them. This is the case even if a surprise sex scene shows up in a movie. This is meant to hook, but really it traumatizes and initiates. So then, how can we wonder where a *spirit spouse* came from? You watch that stuff and without repentance? Then the *spirit*(s) attached to that stuff are now allowed entrance into your house, life, and soul.

This further leads to a silent tethering to the Curse of the Law for all parties and within that curse, poverty. And, if long-standing: Deep Poverty. Can you see now how determined the devil is to rope people into sin, bondage, yokes, even repeating the same evils over and again to make sure a person is captive?

Yes, your poverty or Deep Poverty could be related to your relationship with porn. Even surprise porn. Even porn that "found" you that you didn't type into your search bar. It all has ropes and chains and entanglements meant to trap.

Satan's signature is always the same: expose, shame, accuse, destroy.

But God's pattern is also consistent: cover, restore, redeem, and protect.

If this happened to you or someone you know, you are not the shame. The act done *to* you does not define you. You are not beyond repair. What was uncovered, God can cover again — with righteousness and honor.

You can fight back. Spiritually (with prayer and Truth. Fight back emotionally with community and healing. And, legally through courts and protections, both in the natural and in the Courts of Heaven. Revenge porn is basically digital humiliation that correlates to the old stockades designed to accuse, expose, degrade, shame and possibly control. Revenge porn are those images the devil trots out to remind you of what you did last night, or last summer and to make you cower, or go sit in the corner and stop living your productive abundant life that Jesus died for you to have. The devil may be telling you to go get back on that tree of poverty or tighten the reins of poverty against you and your bloodline, expecting you not to know and declare that Jesus already did that for you. You are redeemed; you are free!

Revenge porn is for *control*. Yes, it is witchcraft, and it is designed to control both the doer and the viewer.

Repent if you played a part in this. Renounce the sin, the porn. Renounce and denounce the association with the demonic, with Satan. Renounce and denounce the entanglements created. You may also have to deal with satanic marriage, satanic soul ties, *spirit spouse* and *spirit children*. All of these things tether people to poverty hell and steals money from them, even if they ever get the chance to think that they are close to breakthrough or payday. Through *spirit spouse* and *spirit children* the devil takes people's money as if they are paying perpetual spiritual alimony and spiritual child support. You've got to get rid of *them* to get rid of him (the devil).

The only way you could even claim complete innocence is if the cameras were hidden and you were with your legally married spouse. However, is your spouse innocent? Or, has your spouse brought demons to your marital bed by their secret behaviors, such as watching porn or secretly filming you? The Bible says that those in a marriage should not defraud one another. However, if you agreed to it, then the devil was already in it as porn is the devil's invention.

Porn actors are Satanists or become such. (They have to; they use the demonic charge for the acts. Porn sex is not normal.)

Things that seem little to us, things that seem innocuous, or things that are "private," secret, or hidden are still things that can tie a man up or even put him in a stockade or on a *tree,* re-binding him to the Curse and especially to poverty as the first sign or lasting sign of that curse is active in his life.

We need to both search ourselves and also listen when one-another ministry is presented to us; perhaps your Christian brother can see what you cannot and can help you be set free, even though Jesus has already made all the arrangements for our deliverance and freedom.

The Redeemer

Jesus wasn't just crucified, He was mocked, stripped, beaten, and displayed. That means that all of what happened in the preceding chapters happened to Him, except there were no cellphones to record the event and no internet yet to post to, in the Earth realm. They divided His clothes tells us that there were no outfits on the Cross. Jesus was exposed on that Tree.

That means the Jesus took the punishment, and also the shame. It also means that He was put in the divine stockade, on a brutal Cross so we could walk free. What do you think that whole display was on the Via Dolorosa and at Golgotha? It was for shame and humiliation. In our times we might call that a *perp walk*. Ultimately, He bore the curse and the humiliation — all of it. A man who could have called 12 legions of angels, did not because of the Love the Father gave Him for us and for His obedience to the Father whom He loved, purely.

> Who for the joy that was set before him endured the cross, **despising the shame**, and is seated at the right hand of the throne of God. (Hebrews 12:2)

Jesus' Passion was one of shame for all of mankind. Even though He was only on the Cross a few hours, the time leading up to it, the indignity was more than an innocent man should have to bear and more than any of us could have borne.

But Jesus did it for us. Everything He did was to untie us from a rope, a chain, a tether to the Curse of the Law, and within that, poverty and Deep Poverty. For those deeply entangled by ancestry and by their own personal sin, choices and iniquity, Jesus did it to untie us from many ropes and to break every chain where we were attached to sin, death, sickness, and poverty.

The shame that meets a bloodline, or a family takes on a new meaning to me as to why Jesus may have sent His own mother,

Mary to another Disciple altogether while He was yet on the Cross. In that culture, a son being crucified? Jesus said, "Son, behold your Mother. Mother, behold your son". Yes, the intention, since Jesus was leaving may have been for that Disciple to take care of Mary, but the awareness of the shame of hanging and death by tree brought to that culture would have been too much. God, through Jesus Christ is well able and famous for the exchange--, the upgrade. By Jesus Christ we all can change bloodlines and foundations, and we can live instead of dying.

> When Jesus therefore saw his mother, and the disciple standing by, whom he loved, he saith unto his mother, Woman, behold thy son! Then saith he to the disciple, Behold thy mother! And from that hour that disciple took her unto his own *home.*
> (John 19:26-27)

And as all the male Disciples were hidden after He died, the moral lesson the Sadducees and Pharisees wanted to impart to the people looked like it had worked. This act was to communicate that *this could happen to you too, if you don't stop believing on this*

Man. This was to bring a halt to Jesus' ministry by shame. Ultimately, it didn't work, did it?

> For I am not ashamed of the gospel of Christ: for it is the power of God unto salvation to every one that believeth; to the Jew first, and also to the Greek.(Romans 1:16)

> For whosoever shall be ashamed of me and of my words, of him shall the Son of man be ashamed, when he shall come in his own glory, and *in his* Father's, and of the holy angels. (Luke 9:26)

But Jesus took the Tree. For us.

> Looking unto Jesus the author and finisher of our faith; who for the joy that was set before him endured the cross, despising the shame, and is set down at the right hand of the throne of God. (Hebrews 12:2)

Jesus took the Tree for us, the shame, the humiliation—the Cross. For the sake of this book let us remain keenly aware that Jesus took the tree for us to be free of poverty--, even Deep Poverty, so why then by sin would we let ourselves get tangled up into the shame of the Curse of the Law ever again?

Then God flips the script: He lets His own Son be hung on a tree, so that every curse, every sin, every unjust judgment, every evil ordinance, — even the ones we carried or committed, even the ones we deserved, could be nailed there and left behind.

Even though those ropes each had a root, every curse has a cure.

But Christ came to **restore what shame tried to erase.** He took all the shame, the public shame, so we can be free of it. Freedom meant untying mankind from shame, from hell, from death, sickness, and poverty.

The Tethering

Christ's taking the public shame is a deliverance for us, yes for our minds, and souls, but it is a deliverance in that it looses us from the shackles of the enemy. Once we are completely unshackled, shall we not walk out or climb out of the pit of Deep Poverty, if that is where the devil has placed us? Now, when a man is untied from that Curse the things he will find to do will prosper instead of being reduced to nothing despite of all his effort.

Christ did the heavy lifting, but we, ourselves must be instrumental in our untethering to the Curse. It may be hard for any person to do that deep dive into their own soul to divide out what is good from what is bad, not making excuses saying, Oh, *that's just the way I am*. Or, *That's just the way that my family is*. By not being able to separate the flesh things especially, the things that hinder or bind a soul from full Godly expression, those things are strongholds, and strangleholds against prosperity.

Especially not being able to let go of sin, even deeply embedded sin, a man holds on to what is holding on to him and what is holding him back and holding him down. So many millions in abject or Deep Poverty in Sub Saharan Africa, for example? The place is riddled with witchcraft, which may have been all they knew or know. It may be the only way they get the little that they have. It may be how they get more than others to have a sense of enough, importance, or honor. It may be how they feel better about themselves or feel better than others. But the deeper sin and iniquity are embedded in a bloodline, the deeper the poverty. Maybe not right away because the devil makes promises and may even keep them to a certain degree, but he always calls in chips sooner or later unless he can continue to get blood sacrifices.

Too many times, the thing a man chooses to do to rid himself of poverty or lack is the thing that ties him more in the spirit to evil and eventually he may find himself or even a relative on a tree, if not today, into his generations. Devil deals are all ropes and chains.

This doesn't just happen in Africa. And it doesn't just happen to Africans. People, be wise. There are people in First World countries still attempting to make deals with the devil. These deals are made by people with **no vision**, no sight or awareness of the future, or that there is a future. These deals are made by people who do not believe they are connected to any other people. They believe the deal they make is separate and apart from all of their relatives, when really they are sinning for the entire family when they make a devil deal. And, such deals that may temporarily get them things they believe they want, but ultimately those "deals" that may appear to gain for them wealth, fame, or power will eventually cost them everything including destruction of their bloodline and all that blood will be on the hands of the human "dealmaker."

The Devil & Trauma

If the devil can traumatize a person deeply, suddenly, chronically he can move that person into survival mode which is a fancy way of saying a person will get *jumped* into their flesh. Fear for example will hijack the thinking mind and the emotional mind will take over. That is when mistakes and poor choices can happen. The person is now operating out of their flesh. In the flesh are tether after tether tying a person, or a bloodline to the devil, to a cascade of works of the flesh, sickness, to captivity, slavery, poverty.

So, even in the natural if someone made a man a sudden millionaire, as in winning the lottery, if they are still tied to poverty and since poverty is spiritual, they may lose everything very suddenly. (Witches call this sweet pain.) There could already be a judgment, a verdict, an evil ordinance that "This man shall remain in poverty." If that man doesn't do the spiritual work, to reverse the judgment and the verdict and take that ordinance and nail it to the Cross of Jesus Christ, whatever he does in the natural, alone, cannot overcome the spiritual.

Capturing people in the spirit or in the natural; does it matter which comes first? If the devil can get at least one evil human agent to agree with his diabolical plots and plans, then his hunting won't be in vain--, he will capture some body. He now can get candidates for vicious rituals, human blood for sacrifice, and people to torment. Declare that neither you nor the people you pray for are candidates for any evil.

While that is happening, those doing the tormenting think they are getting off scot-free, but they are not.

A tactic of war may be to threaten a man's life, threaten everything he believes in and move him into fear mode--, daily. In fear mode or any other survival mode, a man can be manipulated or initiated very easily as he feels his own desperation.

Turned for Good

God is famous for making what I call great exchanges. What the devil means for harm, God turns it around for good, as He did with Joseph. God will teach folks a lesson with the very thing that they idolize or are using for evil, such as each of the plagues that came as an answer to each of the Egyptian *gods* that Pharoah believed in.

Jesus answered her, "If you knew the gift of God and who it is that asks you for a drink, you would have asked him and he would have given you living water. (John 4:10)

Now, watch God flip to the Good News. God can take a bad thing and turn it good. God can use the very thing that is bad and make it good. A curse can become a blessing; nothing is impossible with God. The Serpent was the cause of the original curses in the Garden of Eden, even bringing death, but God told Moses to take a bronze snake and lift it up and when the people look at it, they shall be healed. Jesus, too was lifted up for the healing of mankind and all their woes. Saints of God we must have knowledge to know the difference between images that represent a snake or snakes on a tree, else we may harbor accursed things.

There are four things that represent a snake on a rod or a tree, the first being the bronze snake of Moses. The second represents trickery and it is the caduceus; it has two snakes, not one and represents the staff that the idol *god*, the god of war, Hermes carried.

The Rod of Asclepius has one snake and represents medicine – a lot of doctors may use this as their logo. We hope this was from the incident with Moses and the bronze snake not that doctors wanted a cool looking logo with a snake on it.

The fourth is the real deal, it is Jesus Christ on the Cross of Calvary. However, it is not good to wear or represent Jesus Christ on the Cross because He is no longer on it. But He is the author and finisher of our faith, and He lives! Jesus died so you wouldn't have to go to the Cross or to the tree, so why would you put Him back up there?

> Christ redeemed us from the curse... by becoming a curse for us.(Galatians 3:13)

Specifically, a *tree* in the Garden of Eden helped usher in the Curse of the Law. God then took another Tree--, the Cross on Calvary to redeem the people from that very Curse. Jesus didn't just take your personal sin, He broke the generational disgrace too. He blotted out the handwriting of curses in your family, including poverty and Deep Poverty.

Every curse stops at the Cross of Jesus Christ. The shame doesn't have to be inherited. But you can't just wish it away or decide that you won't inherit it – you must do something spiritually about it. The family line can be **healed and restored** but there are conditions. Salvation, conversion, and stop all the flesh acts; they are tethering folks back into sin and back to the devil and his system which is sickness, poverty and eternal damnation.

Even in modern times, in many cultures, including African American, Indigenous, and immigrant communities, the public death or disgrace of a family member brings ongoing suspicion, social isolation, and economic disenfranchisement. Some families are still living under shame that started with something one ancestor did, or something they had done to them. The curse on a family affects the entire family in the natural socially, economically, spiritually. In this sense, the perpetrator, whether living or dead, is not judged alone since there is the issue of family honor—or dishonor.

Man attempts to break this by moving from place to place--, for a fresh start, where no one knows them, and they can pretend to be normal or believe they will be treated differently or better if no one knows them. But this is spiritual, wherever you go, the *spirits* you are trying to outrun will get there before you do. And there they are just waiting. Their job is also to influence people and situations to treat you a certain way – the very same way you've always been treated, most likely. No matter where you live or move to.

Only a stronger Spirit, a stronger and greater altar can break this dark assignment, that is hinged on an evil verdict against that man. That greatest altar is Jesus Christ.

So, when a mob, for example, hanged a man on a tree, they were trying to act as if they had the power to try, judge, and execute, attempting to step into the position of God. When they hanged a man, they were trying also to malign, sideline and curse that man and his bloodline. Any murder accomplishes this, of course, but especially the grievous spectacle of hanging by tree or gallows.

Haman wanted to hang Mordecai to humiliate and make despondent all the Jews or as many as possible.

The curse of humiliation and shame, must be broken spiritually and Jesus has the power to break it. He broke the tree curse with a *tree* of His own. With Christ a hanging can become a C-hanging, if we appropriate it for ourselves.

Remember, there's bloodline and bloodline connections and there is the potential for collective captivity. Folks, when a door is open to a bloodline it is open. Depending on whom in the bloodline opened it will have bearing on how easy or difficult it will be to close that door. Also, when it was opened, how long it has been opened has bearing on how difficult it will be to overcome and close that door. Once whatever *spirits* or strongholds came in through that open door get into the third generation, it's deeply embedded in the foundation.

By taking the Tree, hanging on that Tree, Jesus extended redemption to **everyone**. Not just anyone or someone or some ones--, but everyone. Those who would receive spiritual redemption.

The Curse of hanging on a tree, if it were one man and not his whole family, but don't think that wasn't done also. Even if the hanging was for that one person, usually, but the stigma was spiritual and generational. In ancient Hebrew society, when someone was executed by hanging or displayed on a tree, it meant They were under divine judgment. Their names, family, and bloodline were stained.

When this was done illegally, it was meant to appear as if God had the victim under divine judgment, to both attempt to sanction the criminals doing the hanging and killing, as well as send an evil message to the family and throughout the land, implying that God was in agreement with their evil. And, it was a vain attempt to sanctify, whitewash the actions of the mob who did the hanging if this was an illegal lynching.

What *god*?

The little g *god* they served, obviously. Not Jehovah.

The *curse* itself wasn't automatically passed down like a virus, unless it was from parent to child or grandchild. But the consequences and perception could affect the entire family of even distant relatives.

Spiritually, if not repented of or broken, that disgrace could open legal doors for generational bondage.

A man sins. Then the devil runs with an Evil Petition to the Courts of Heaven where he accuses men day and night to try to get a judgment against that man. Whatever the outcome, it's written down. If the family is not spiritual, they may have no clue of what was written against them or that anything was written in indelible, spiritual ink. They may just wag their heads at their wayward relative, turn from the spectacle and keep living, because, *that boy was always trouble anyway.* In so doing they may neglect seeking remedy for what the devil just recorded against the entire bloodline. As well they may neglect to go into the Courts of Heaven and answer that petition or open up their own petition that the devil be precluded from roping them all into the rope that hung their relative.

Just as Jesus went into the Wilderness to seek and save the very least so that not even one was lost, can we not do the same within our own families? Of course, providing that the "lost" or wayward in a family will hear and follow Christ.

For example, someone is executed for idolatry or sorcery, their children may suffer rejection, accusation and poverty, repeating the same sin cycles because a spiritual *door* was opened and never closed. When altars get fired up, even evil altars, they keep emanating evil until a greater altar stops it and breaks up that altar.

In Biblical language, "everyone" meant the one hanging, and because of spiritual laws entire bloodlines were affected. In Deuteronomy, the curse applied to the one who was hanged, but in God's economy, bloodlines are spiritual highways. What one generation does can activate or trigger effects in the next.

> Visiting the iniquity of the fathers on the children to the third and fourth generation of those who hate Me. (Exodus 20:5)

The curse isn't just about the act or the lone actor, even if he is a criminal, since all of us have sinned and fallen short of the Glory of God. But it is also about the unrepented bloodline connection. This means that a father's curse can touch the child, unless that curse is broken, dismantled, and removed.

The act of hanging someone wasn't just execution, it could label a family with lasting spiritual consequences and social shame. **Shame can be a direct link to poverty.** Galatians 3:13 isn't just theological — it is a profound legal statement and truth in the spiritual realm.

Jesus <u>became</u> the cursed One *for us*. He took our generational baggage, our inherited disgrace, and our bloodline bondage, and nailed it to the Cross. Jesus <u>became</u> the curse and then covered the Curse – all curses with His own perfect, precious Blood. Jesus broke the chain and cycle and punishment of sin, not so we could sin again, but so we could live. The cycle isn't always automatic, and it may skip generations. However, if the door is ajar or open, it may allow the devil in when he wants in, unless someone closes it. Jesus broke sickness and disease off of us. He broke poverty, even Deep Poverty and brought us an abundant life.

When Christ hung on *His* tree, He didn't just redeem you, He went into your bloodline, dug up the root curses, and offered full reversal. The Spirit of God transcends all space and time. I think to fully grasp this, you should meditate on this for a while. Jesus can go back and forth in time and in your bloodline and fix everything that is broken, even Deep Poverty.

So now you get to say:

- The curse ends with me.
- I plead the bloodline of Jesus over my family line.
- The tree that cursed my house is now healed by a greater, more powerful, Godly Tree--, the Tree at Golgotha is now the tree that heals it.

If your faith is stronger, you can say, The Cross is the Tree that has already healed it.

God Sends a Deliverer

God sends a deliverer on every level. In a family. To a city. To a Nation.

The Lord will not leave you comfortless or hopeless. He is full of Mercy and compassion. Unless you or a people have been turned over to a reprobate mind, God will send help from the sanctuary; He will send help in the form of deliverance.

Joseph was sent to deliver Jacob's family from famine, and hence, death. Jacob didn't reject the deliverance, but the 10 older brothers did. They didn't see that they would need deliverance either now, soon, or in the future, number one. But they didn't see that deliverance was the issue at all. By the time we get a clue and call for help, we are in God's yesterday because He has already prepared and sent the deliverer for us. Wasn't the Lamb already slain before the foundation of the world? That was thousands of years before the New Testament, but God had already answered. So, unless and until we learn how to think inside and outside of Time, how will we possibly even know the Mind of God?

It could be the voice of a friend, or even a stranger that says the one thing to you that sets you free or puts you on the path for your deliverance. But if you disdain Wisdom, Knowledge and even words of correction, then you could miss God.

I hadn't seen a regular patient for more than a year and a half. One day, he returned for a cleaning. I asked him where he had been. For the past year and a half, he said because of relentless headaches he had seen a neurologist, an ENT doctor, and many other kinds of medical specialists who had run many tests on him. He mentioned that it was both time-consuming and expensive. Finally, his diagnosis was given to my patient by all these medical by asking him, "Has anyone ever told you that you grind your teeth?"

He said, "Yes, my dentist, a couple of years ago, but I don't pay any attention to her."

By hearing Joseph's dreams, they saw the results of deliverance not for themselves but for the deliverer, Joseph would receive honor.

By rejecting the deliverer, the people are saying, *We don't want him or her to have honor.* **We** want the honor, or we want <u>no</u> honor in our family, city or nation.

Jacob's boys were blind to the entire issue of the purpose or the act behind Joseph receiving honor – as if people just get honor for no reason at all? Of the ten older brothers of Joseph, even with their spiritual gifts they were not sharp enough to see into the future to see that Joseph would be solving a huge problem and he would be acknowledged for that. They also didn't realize that if God was bestowing the honor on Joseph, or anyone for that matter then that person must be in the Will of God and doing what they were sent to Earth to do. Did they not realize that if it were to be a great deal of honor then the purpose that Joseph, for example, had to fulfill might be dangerous, treacherous, very difficult? Did they not think that if God gave Joseph a dream that an assignment accompanied it and if they interfered with Joseph, they'd be interfering with the plans of God? Ten of them together couldn't figure that out?

Worry about yourself? These grown men didn't, they worried about the dreams of their kid brother.

I am in no way saying that any or everyone that was ever waylaid, stalled, stopped, derailed or killed prematurely was a deliverer for mankind, but that person was sent here to Earth with purpose. They may have been a deliverer for their own family or community. Whatever they had to offer, based on why God sent them here was cut short or cut off entirely if they suffered premature death. But the expression of public disgrace such as hanging speaks to the evil hearts and mind behind the act.

When God sends a deliverer He usually sends someone who will do anything for you as that person is obeying his mandate from God. That person is not God, but is ordained and sent by God. When you disrespect that person, you disrespect God.

People who carry honor have no problem with another person receiving honor. It is those with no honor that are sniveling petty types who do not want anyone else to have honor. Yet, from the onset, man was crowned with glory and honor. This could be why people can be so captive with a newborn baby and cherish him or her so dearly – until they sin. After sin, glory and honor is lost. Now, we see folks begin to feel a little differently about this new sinner.

Until that first sin, most in a family will do too much to lift that child up, bragging on him or her. New babies even smell better than those who take on a new funk after sin.

God is not like that – He doesn't look on sin. He hates sin, but not the sinner, especially the sinner who is repentant in their heart.

Hating Your Deliverer

Marvel not if they hate you, they hated Me first. (John 15:18)

People don't usually hate someone of a like mind or a like spirit. So why did they hate Jesus? Because they were of their father, the devil. As Jesus was walking around Galilee, Bethlehem, Judea, Capernaum and everywhere else He went wearing His Glory and Honor. When the glory-less and the honor less sees Glory and honor on another man he is both jealous and covetous if he greedy, and especially if he has lost his own. Pharisees, Sadducees may have been walking, talking examples of this.

Well folks, you guessed it – one who is sent by God will have glory and honor on their heads. We've already realized how easily some reject such a person either because it brings them under conviction as they realized their own filthiness or they just don't want another person to have glory and honor, or either glory or honor. But when they have both? Well, Yes and Amen.

They don't just hate their individual deliverer, they often hate the deliverer of the people, the nations. Until they don't. Until they see what's in it for them or they can move that deliverer to the position of idol, for idol worship.

Moses, the people complained, "You brought us out here to die?" Hey, die as a slave or die free, which is better? Which is worse?

You think you're so much--- when a person knows who they are and exhibits confidence--, many don't like that.

Wisdom is a deliverer. Wisdom is the correct application of Knowledge, and it can deliver. The knowledge that the man in the previous chapter grinds his teeth extensively and getting a mouth guard would have either delivered him or at least mitigated the damage done to his teeth and body, but he rejected it and wasted years of time and thousands of dollars while suffering in pain.

Knowledge. If people perish for a lack of knowledge, then by Knowledge shall people be saved or not perish. Paul said he didn't know he was a sinner until the Law was preached to him.

Instruction; do not hate instruction.

Fear of the LORD is the beginning of Wisdom, it is the beginning of knowledge, it is deliverance. Appreciation and study of the Word of God will deliver. Faith comes by hearing--, read the Word out loud; demons hate that, and it will build up your faith. Praise, worship, time in the presence of God. Corporate prayer as well as individual prayer and praying in the Spirit will all bring or help bring deliverance.

Worship includes sacrifice at a Godly altar to bring or facilitate deliverance, even from poverty. In the way that God uses exchange, look well to how your little bit of money can be exchanged on a Godly altar for God's more than enough or more than you have room enough to receive. But know this: In the middle of receiving abundance there is the other spiritual step of being loosed from evil yokes, stockades and untangled and untied from evil trees. Jesus already did this exchange for us, but like Juneteeth our slow, slow flesh may not have gotten the message yet and a man's iniquity or unrepented sin may have roped a man back into that same bondage.

Coveting Honor

When a man by his own flesh attempts to get his lost honor back, or steal someone else's as not to look so honor less and guilty himself we will find him coveting honor.

When a man wants power, he will covet what others have, their honor, their glory, their money, position, authority or goods. This is why men go to war. This is why, even kings go to war.

When a person is seeking fame, they may scorch the Earth to try to take the power that God has imbued in a person (or group) for oneself than allow it to be used for another, others, or everyone—for the common good. That man is selfish, self-centered and a narcissist. Will a man rob God? Lucifer tried to rob God of Worship in Heaven. We know what happened to him.

Saul was covetous of David's greater charge and greater anointing and so wanted to kill David because of jealousy.

Haman hated the Jews and wanted to exterminate them even though they were God's chosen people.

Herod was jealous of Jesus' star, and wanted to kill him. Later, the Pharisees and Sanhedrin Council were jealous of Jesus' following, authority, and power.

The insecure man thinks or says, If I can't have the most, then maybe I can have more than the next guy. If that becomes a reality, then more than the next guy becomes more than the next guy after that.

All the devil has to do is incite the lust of a man, or many men, and those men, by fighting to have more and more or the most will AGREE with the devil to steal, kill and destroy to take away from another man, or as many men as possible.

The greedy man does not seem to realize that his own greed will affect not only other people but the balance of things in general.

The devil may incite a man's desire for more, or the *most* and call it honor – misnaming Greed, Lust, evil, dissensions, and every other work of the flesh. While the person seeking for more, more, and the *most* will believe that misnomer of calling covetousness other than what it is because it may help him justify his evil or ease his conscience.

> Remove far from me vanity and lies: give me neither poverty nor riches; feed me with food convenient for me. (Proverbs 30:8)

With the mindset from the above verse in Proverbs, a person will never agree with the devil or sin against God when it comes to material goods.

Why do men want to be honored? Seen? Heard?

Idolatry.

Celebrities want attention, fame, honor from men, money, power, and etcetera. They want manmade versions of Glory & Honor. Man was made for glory and honor. Man was made to carry glory and honor. Man was crowned with glory and honor, but the first sin strips it. Once he realizes it is gone, he wants that glory and honor back, but he intends to get it either in the flesh or by some other crooked means.

Enter the devil.

For example, that precious child who sins and now loses glory in their parents' eyes may now resort to diabolical means to get that glory back, by trying to steal it or by upstaging their sibling. Constantly. This could be how and why sibling rivalries start.

I take great pleasure in writing about Jesus' temptation in the Wilderness because now there is a new revelation on it. All the things the devil was offering Jesus were the manmade, facsimile, substitute versions of Earth Glory and Earth honor. However, dear friends, Jesus had not lost His original and real, genuine and spiritual God-given Glory and Honor, so what must those trinkets and baubles really have looked like to Jesus?

Oh, if we could see the temptations of Earth and this life in the same way we'd never make a demonic trade or covet what another person has.

We Will Do It Our Way

Why is poverty in the Curse of the Law? Folks when sin happens the consequences are sickness, poverty, and death. Poverty is in there because it is. God said that Adam would now toil and the ground wouldn't cooperate with him—for a agrarian society, that meant poverty.

The wages of sin is death… (Romans 6:23)

Why poverty? Because when one sins the result is spiritual death. The person is now **dead**, so what do they need money for? But the person is not dead in the natural, they are still walking and talking and moving around. Yup. But until repentance, they are **spiritually dead**. Like vultures coming to clean a carcass, money, wealth, material possessions that the skeleton is clinging to are taken away, subtly, suddenly or even violently. The same is true for sickness, but we are focusing on poverty in this book. If you are on the way out of the Earth realm, what do you need money for? You can't take it with you. So, the demonic oppressions and punishments that come with unrepented sin are the things the devil is known for--, steal, kill, and destroy. Who easier to steal from than a dead person?

I challenge you today, if you are being ripped off all the time, everywhere you go, then you need to repent. Ask God for Mercy, and ask God if you are even spiritually alive. If you are spiritually alive, then you can be naturally alive. If you are not spiritually alive, then --, no wonder.

And you hath he quickened, who were dead in trespasses and sins. (Ephesians 2:1)

Spiritual death has to be reversed and quickened spiritually, in Christ Jesus. This is not a matter of fixing a small problem in the hospital OR on the operating table.

So, if a bloodline has been spiritually dead long enough whether they refuse to make deals with the devil, or honor the deals already made, that they may not even know anything about, here comes the poverty or even Deep Poverty. The embedding of poverty into a bloodline can be subtle or sudden. It could be ancient. Someone in your bloodline may have been into witchcraft or satanism and dedicated your whole bloodline, but you know nothing about it.

Deep Poverty would result from that.

Nearly everything that a person tries to do to change their condition in life is met with opposition or failure. They remain in Deep Poverty. This is not by chance. This is embedded spiritually in their bloodline and foundation. Work your fingers to the bone? No matter what you do in your flesh, eve with good intentions and a good attitude, that is not how you fight and defeat this.

Here are some more flesh moves: Maybe we can just *look* like we're delivered? We can get some new stuff, cars, clothes, jewelry, and house this way we will not look impoverished. We can remove this shame.

Folks, that means we want to manipulate the spiritual situation we find ourselves in by flesh works, and that unfortunately means more flesh. We want to attain the trappings that make us look (or feel) successful. This can begin the image-driven life. A man may rationalize and say I've been working hard, I like nice things, I want nice things, and I'm tired of waiting.

Without Christ and the Blood of Jesus, sin will be employed to cover up sin.

So, he may acquire things to enhance his image or make his emotions, pride or greed feel good. Some of these acquisitions may come at a **price higher than what he thought.** For his image he may reach for baubles that are dangled in front of him, or they are the things that everyone else has.

In the flesh dwells no good thing according to my Bible, so let's look at Jack and the Beanstalk. Jack traded the money for the cow for magic seeds. Well, that's the first problem, Jack is already delving into magic which is from the dark side in order to solve a problem that has tied him to poverty. This is a problem that is being enforced by the dark side.

The first problem is that the dark side can't save you from the dark side. Just about overnight, with these magic seeds, Jack grew a beanstalk--, yes, Jack grew a tree. Jack climbed the tree and there he saw a goose that laid golden eggs. Jack coveted the golden egg but there was a giant (a strongman).

When a man sees a thing but doesn't get to have that thing, the devil is involved. God would never torment a man like that. Jack is almost there. But if he can get that egg, which – is it really his? Or is he now stealing?

However, guarding this goose and these eggs either because it all belonged to him, or there were certain evil covenants to tether Jack and his mother to poverty and Jack didn't know jack about them. So in his flesh he sought out magic. In his strength he climbed a beanstalk. In his lust he reached for that golden egg. The spiritual strongman came after Jack, but Jack didn't have jack to fight him with. (I know that's not how the fairytale ends, but his is just for example.)

Fear and other survival-mode based works of the flesh may put a person in desperation causing them to make costly mistakes such as committing crimes to remedy their situation. (read my book series, **Upgrade: How to Get Out of Survival Mode**).

It's really quite a game the devil is playing, if in the spirit a man is tethered, then how will he be able to accomplish or receive the things that he must in the natural get in order to prosper his life?

When man goes into his flesh to try to solve a spiritual problem. in the Old Testament there were two particular women at different times, interfacing with different prophets who solved their poverty problems **spiritually**. And that was the correct remedy.

So, I am saying that poverty on any level didn't just "happen." There was a plan. There was a meeting. There was an accusation, and a judgment passed ad then things started to happen to cause poverty to come into a man's life and into his bloodline or in that community, state, or nation.

Why am I saying all of this? Because a person may be cursed or forcefully put under the Curse of the Law and taking no recourse whatsoever to stop the curse and avail himself to Jesus Christ's work at Calvary for redemption and salvation. This could be why there is poverty in a life, even Deep Poverty that has endured for several or many generations in a bloodline.

In the spirit, one could be spiritually dead--, does he even know it? In the spirit, one could be hanging on a Tree, when Jesus already did that for us so we could come down from the curse, or up from the pit, or ever where your soul has been locked away to keep you from wealth and wealth from you. Whatever has been done to make you desperate, ignorant, foolish, greedy, to keep you tied up in the devil's prison, to keep you in poverty – there is redemption for that. We need Knowledge and Wisdom and Mercy and Grace to untie us so we can be free.

The tree—the Cross of Jesus Christ, an emblem of suffering and shame. Hymn written by George Bernard,

On a hill far away, stood an old rugged
Cross. The emblem of suff'ring and shame
And I love that old Cross where the dearest
and best
For a world of lost sinners was slain

Things that Tend to Poverty

Read my book, ***the spirit of poverty***...

Things that tend to poverty are just that--, at first. Then there is the second generation and beyond and those things that tie a person or a family or people group to poverty become strongholds.

We often think of bonds and chains and yokes tying mankind to the enemy, but I would like to present that it could be the flesh of a man that ties him to sin, to yokes and creates ties and bondages. Like quicksand, the more movement there is the more the person may sink. Wouldn't it be like the devil to come up with such a system? And wouldn't it be like man to think that the thing that got him into the situation could get him out? And isn't that just like gambling?

But, wouldn't it be like God to tell us the answer to getting out of bondage? And wouldn't it be like God to make the solution so simple?

Walk after the Spirit and this way you will not fulfill the works of the flesh.

Stop working the flesh because it is the flesh that ties a man to his enemy.

In ancient times, many cruel kings would punish a man guilty of murder by strapping the man that he allegedly killed to the perpetrator's back--, until the perpetrator actually himself died a slow and painful death. It was a work of the flesh that killed the victim in the first place. Therefore, the flesh act of the murderer tied him to his sin. Unapologetically and hopelessly.

It is quite obvious that the flesh of the murdered man can not extricate the murderer from his judgment. Yet humans often think the thing they did that got them into the trouble – if that is repeated then the trouble will be eradicated.

The gambler thinks the $20 he just lost ta the roulette table – another $20 can get that $20 back as if cash money is bait for other money and this is a fishing expedition.

The point? Deep Poverty cannot be conquered by doing the same things you did to get into it. Deep Poverty cannot be overcome by doing the same things your ancestors did to get into it and that also roped you into it. Something different has to be done. Something in the flesh was done to create the problem, that flesh act translated into a spiritual infraction which translated into a spiritual judgment, which then translated into spiritual punishment, which then translated into a physical punishment.

Money, having money, getting money is not the solution to poverty. Having money of course, mitigates poverty and it makes the sequelae of poverty go slower, but it is not the sole solution. Poverty is spiritual; therefore, something spiritual has to be done to correct it.

Give that man a fish? Teach that man to fish? No matter how many fish he has or gets there is a spiritual force, almost always unseen working to take that fish from that man. Solving that evil spiritual operation, and the issues that allow it--, that is the solution to ending poverty.

Jesus knew. God sent Him here to do that spiritual thing to get us out of poverty. It's in the Bible, so shall we not also know it? What is peculiar to your bloodline you must discern it or ask the Holy Spirit and then make that change, do that thing, or stop doing that thing. That is your act of resisting the devil or devils that insist on poverty and Deep Poverty in your life.

If we recount again how this poverty happened, we will see out of five steps, three of them are spiritual steps--, the most is happening in the spirit. Only the bookends, Step One and Step Five are flesh steps. So, if you don't believe that poverty is spiritual, then can you see that it is 3/5 spiritual? That is 60%, and that is a predominance of the steps. You must find out the spiritual reasons you or your family is impoverished and take the appropriate spiritual steps such as fasting and prayer, and repentance.

It's Spiritual

It's spiritual, so the flesh way won't work, however being spiritual doesn't mean that there is nothing to do in the natural. It's not magic. It's spiritual.

"Your way" is governed by what you can see. Your way is informed by what you can sense with your five natural senses or what other carnal, five-sensed people know or can see or tell you about. Your way is entangled in flesh and that most likely will be five things out of five will be flesh acts. No surprise that there are five natural senses. In reality, since it is spiritual the three of the five steps need to be spiritual steps.

Your way is spiritually set, like cement clogging up and locking up your foundation. It is spiritual. It could be without realizing it you are working *with* the enemy that is working against you to keep you tethered, chained, fettered, bound and yoked in poverty.

We need Jesus. We need spiritual discernment, Wisdom, Truth, Mercy, Grace and divine rescue, actually. If we could do it ourselves and by ourselves, the why did Jesus come to Earth?

Continuing to repeat and do the same things that either got you into bondage or keeps you there, further empowers the enemy and embeds poverty into a person's life. But this person cannot stop by sheer willpower. First, he may have no will power to stop it; there is an evil anointing that makes him or drives him to repeat dangerous behaviors, creating destructive cycles. it can't be helped until one is delivered from the individual, generational, familial, and ancestral strongholds.

What are the strongholds in your family? Ask the Lord what are the things that you may be doing that are counterproductive to wealth and prosperity.

The following may promote deliverance from poverty and promote prosperity, although it is not an exhaustive list.

- Wisdom Builds Her house but the foolish tears it down. Not seeking Wisdom keeps poverty around. We don't worship education, but we do seek Wisdom and knowledge from God. We seek it God's way, not by divination.
- Cheerful giving and generosity tend to prosperity.
- Remembering God -He gives us power to get wealth
- Careful stewardship
- Worship and all other disciplines of the faith and resisting evil.
- Not being ashamed of the Gospel
- Faith pleases God; when God is pleased, we see prosperity.
- Spiritual Mapping – searching your family bloodline to see why things are as they are and why your people behave or misbehave as they do.

Spiritual warfare. When victories are won, God gives reward, spoils of every kind. God will give what you need, want, and ask for.

The converse will welcome and keep poverty (also not an exhaustive list):

- Blatant or Hidden sin
- Pride and other works of the flesh.
- Chronic, unrepentant sin.
- Mischief: laying traps for others
- False balance in business: cheating others.
- Illegal sex.
- Idolatry.
- Witchcraft. Spewing curses.
- Practicing or participating in any abomination--, anything the Lord hates.

Don't Reject Your Deliverer

When you reject the deliverer that the Lord has sent to you, you reject your deliverance. Your deliverer is spiritual. Your deliverer is *sent* and also is imbued with spiritual gifts, powers, skills, abilities, and anointing. Your meeting anyone that God sends into your life from a real friend to a destiny helper, to a spouse or your actual deliverer is by divine appointment.

If you are one who feels that you never have any help or have never encountered a destiny helper, it could be that the devil has got you in a wrong timeline so you are in the wrong places at wrong times to meet the right people. Yup, something else to pray about: Destiny clocks, divine timing of God and divine connections and appointments.

If you want to think of it in the natural, let's say you need something fixed at your house and a guy comes to do that job for you but brings no tools. Will the thing get fixed?

Let's say there is no guy to fix anything, but a box of tools arrives at your house, but you don't know how to use them and have no authority to use them. Will that thing get fixed? So you meet people, but they are not the right people, so they do not offer you what you need or what you are praying to God about.

Someone from Comcast called me and said I could get a new router or modem and it was free of charge. I thought, okay, that will make my services run better? Great, send it. Two weeks later the box sits unopened because I don't feel like thinking about it, looking at it, figuring it out or even changing anything.

Isn't that so human of me?

In the meantime, my internet seems to be working fine so why change it? If it's slow, I've gotten used to it, so why should I change anything? However, now Comcast is calling me asking for their old equipment back that is still attached to my system. They are now threatening me – something about lost or stolen equipment. I'm thinking about sending the new thing back to them in the unopened box. Comcast is saying, hey--, if you're not using it, do you even have it? Where is it? If that device will deliver me from struggle or trouble, then why am I not using it?

The poverty of get-up-and-go, get up and get it done is still a form of poverty. It's a poverty of the mind. Updating my systems when what I need is right there before me is not good. If I don't feel technologically able to attempt the tear down and the new set up, that's a mental issue of laziness or complacency.

Now, some of us are from the time period when service people came to your home, brought equipment and tools with them, and connected things for you. That's what we want when it comes to prayers, deliverance and the things of God, but that is not the way it always is.

In spiritual matters, even if you have someone who has the knowledge, the tools, the anointing and the time to get things done for you, can you just call, tell them to come over or book an appointment and go to their office and they do all the spiritual things that you need done, for you?

The Centurion knew he could tell Jesus, "Just send the Word and my servant will be healed." Well, saints of God, you have authority to use the Word of God. By virtue of this Biblical account the Word has already been *sent*. Now, as God teaches you to war and do battle --, it could be that God is waiting for **you** to send the Word, **yourself**. God may not be waiting for you to find the right person to pray with you, pray for you, or meet with you to heal you or your wallet. God may be waiting for you to shake off the insecurity and the shame and SEND the WORD yourself and be delivered. The Word will deliver and in your capable hands and mouth in your authority, you may be your own deliverer.

Do not reject your deliverer; do not reject yourself. Do not let insecurity, shame or feelings of inadequacy cause you to reject yourself.

Even if someone helps you now, there still will come a time when you **must** know how to handle some spiritual things yourself. We stay in our own lanes, we walk in our own authority, but we are not helpless in spiritual matters. There will come a time when you should be able to do, teach others and also pray for others who are not able to pray for themselves.

If a pastor, prophet, apostle, deliverance minister, intercessor, watchman or a praying best buddy would dig you out of deep poverty so you wouldn't have to do it yourself, how long do you think that would take? If those of the five-fold and other ministry gifts of the Body of Christ were doing that, wouldn't there be a line around every church in the world? Wouldn't people be doing this on a regular basis? Wouldn't there be mass deliverance for Deep Poverty in churches since 700 million people live in poverty in the world, and poverty is both painful and deadly? A Deep Poverty problem seems to be something individuals will have to do for themselves, because it is so deep, entangled and complex. Else some pastors, prophets, apostles, intercessors and some grandmas could have prayed it out of the Earth already. Don't lose heart, the prayers of another may get you started but it may not be the deep deliverance you and your bloodline may need.

Why?

It could be that every tendril of **flesh** that you activate daily and or nightly re-ties or tightens you to the bondage of poverty or Deep Poverty. By *flesh* I mean the stuff you do without thinking, the things you do every day, the things you feel entitled to do—get angry, stay angry, tell white lies, let your eyes rove where they should not, lust, greed, illegal sex, or covetousness. Those are things that YOU must put a stop to in yourself, or nobody's prayers can do very much for you. You must repent, yield to the Word and if your human OS (operating system) is running by an outside entity, **you've** got to be the one to fight it—daily, nightly, until it is defeated and its bindings have to let you, your generations, and your bloodline go.

As said, it is part of the enemy's tactics to make you hate, disregard, disrespect and or shun your deliverer. Only by discernment will you see the truth and override the lies and break the strongholds.

> And in the morning, It will be foul weather to day: for the sky is red and lowring. O ye hypocrites, ye can discern the face of the sky; but can ye not discern the signs of the times? And in the morning, It will be foul weather to day: for the sky is red and lowring. (Matthew 16:3)

You know the sky is lowering, but you've missed your visitation. Let's not know that we are supposed to act up or retaliate against a perceived hurt in the natural, but not discern *spiritual* things. That is how humans get caught up

Years ago, Verizon called to tell me that I needed to change my analog office Internet line or they would be dismantling my line by Friday. I said, "I must keep the same phone number, it's the same number this business has had for 20 years, it cannot be changed". So, the lady on the phone decided to *help* me and she said, "Okay, we can take it down voluntarily and then you wait two weeks, and we can then put the internet line back up and so you will keep the same line.

I agreed and they took the line down. Two weeks came and went—no internet, which meant no billing and a hold on a lot of other things, but we were still open for business. Finally at the beginning of the third week I called Verizon but the person who answered the phone said that they had the order to take the internet line down but not to bring it back up.

What!

So, I asked her to send a technician out and she said, "We don't do that anymore.

We will set everything up and in three days, you will have to connect it yourself."

I didn't know how to do that. So, I looked for a tech who could. I could not find one person who knew how to do this, even though five people tried, and two of them were computer savvy on their full-time jobs. No one from an internet serving company could come for three more weeks-- so I had to figure it out myself and did it myself.

Even though God sends help from the sanctuary, even though there are divine connections all the time, this does not mean that if God has something that you must do that, He will send a "technician" to do it for you. Some things you **must** do <u>yourself</u> as God teaches your hands to battle and your fingers to fight. Wires, cables, cords, ropes, chains--, how long will it take to undo all that if your bloodline is spiritually hog-tied? Sure, God can change it in an instant, but in your deliverance, there should also be a change in you so you learn and grow from it, —so it doesn't happen again, and you go back into that bondage or worse. You may have to sit down and detangle all those threads **YOURSELF** with Help of the Holy Spirit, asking, what is in me or my blood that has attracted poverty and won't let it go?

It could be that in the case of deep poverty **you** will need deep deliverance, and it could be that **you** are along with the Holy Spirit, your own deliverer. There could be so many wires and cables and ties to ancient altars and generational iniquity, and innocent looking booby traps in your own home that only you can figure out what must be done to be rid of Deep Poverty. It could take weeks, months, or years to sort out all those wires, cables, tethers, and ropes.

No church service lasts years. Most deliverance ministers don't pray for only one person during a service. One-on-one meetings could even take years. YOU must be instrumental in your own deliverance. Know this: the salvation of the Lord also includes deliverance from poverty--, poverty of all kinds, every description, from every source and of any duration. God gives us power to get wealth so that He may establish covenant with us (Deuteronomy 8:18), so if we are saved then we walk in an established covenant with the Lord by virtue of many things, one of which is not being broke.

Jesus already hung on that Tree, so why are you back up in it? In the Lord's Salvation could we be spiritual enough to appropriate the blessings of health and healing and being out of poverty? These are markers. These are signs that you belong to God. Surely God, who they say bragged on Job, isn't saying, **Oh, the broke, busted, disgusted and sick ones—they are mine**. Is that how you would brag on your children?

Why and how has the enemy roped your bloodline into this bondage? Why is your family's head in a yoke as in a stockade, shaming, embarrassing, humiliating and holding your people back? Jesus already set you free and in God's way--, He did it **in advance. It is done**. Now, you get to catch up with God's timing where your life is perfected and you have good successes. Sit down if you have to and detangle all the mess that your ancestors and maybe also you have created so you and your bloodline can at last get down of the devil's tree and live.

If you are the one in your generation that God has chosen as the deliverer of your bloodline--, don't think you are the first. I believe that the Lord God has put a deliverer in every generation of every family. However, if your bloodline is still suffering then someone either didn't do what they should have done in the spiritual warfare department, or they may have done nothing, or worked the flesh even more to dig your bloodline **deeper** into poverty.

It could be that the one who was sent to deliver a family is the one they shunned. Didn't they do that to Joseph?

But, saint of God, if God says you are the *chosen* one – don't let that go to your head. It means that you've got a lot of deep spiritual work to do. Congratulations because if God chose you--, many are called, but few are chosen. If God is in this with you, you will be victorious. Kudos to your bloodline because when you are set free, you will be free indeed. You, your family and bloodline should be something that God can brag about, if He wants to.

Be sure you do not listen to the angry mob--, whoever that may be, the many evil voices coming at you on any given day, evil human agents, anyone who is not trying to build you up in the things of God may be trying to tear you down. The evil mob will run you up that Tree. Don't go. Even though we all have sinned and fallen short of the Glory of God and we deserve to be on that Tree instead of Jesus, He has already paid it all for us. So don't let guilt, shame, and an angry mob run you back up that tree,

Repent and run to God. The name of the Lord is a high tower, the righteous run into it and they are saved. Be sure also to teach and pray for all in your bloodline so they don't make the same mistakes again.

With long life I will satisfy him and show him My salvation. (Psalm 91:16)

Prayers

Lord, am I alive spiritually?

Lord, quicken me. Make me alive again that I may move, breathe, and have being, in the Name of Jesus.

Lord, if I am a sinner, hear my cries of repentance and pleas for Mercy.

If I am none of Yours ,give me a Godly sorrow for my sins and a repentant heart and make me one of Yours, in the Name of Jesus.

I seal these words, decrees, declarations and prayers across every dimension, age, era, epoch, timeline, past, present, and future, to infinity. I seal them with the Blood of Jesus and the Holy Spirit of Promise, in the Name of Jesus.

Any retaliation against the author, reader, anyone saying or praying these words, or anyone who will ever pray these prayers, decrees and declarations in the future – Lord let that retaliation be rendered null and void and return with Fire on the head of the perpetrator without Mercy and to infinity, in the Name of Jesus.

Amen. *Thank You, Lord. Hallelujah!*

Dear Reader

Thank you for acquiring and reading this book. Thank you for supporting this ministry.

I pray that you will never be strung up by poverty or Deep Poverty, and that you will never lack knowledge, in the Name of Jesus, Amen.

Shalom,

Dr. Marlene Miles

Important Notes:

More prayers on many topics including healing your foundation, prayers against poverty, prayers for business, prayers against spirit spouse, spirit children can be found on Warfare Prayer Channel on You Tube. https://www.youtube.com/@warfareprayerchannel3853

Teaching and prayers on Dr. Marlene Miles You Tube Channel. https://www.youtube.com/@drmiles8271

The following list is the Dr. Marlene Miles book library. All books are available on Amazon, Kindle, and many are available on other platforms as well.

Prayerbooks by this author

While most books by this author have prayer points either throughout the book or at the end, there are some books that are only prayers. You just open up the book and pray.

Prayers Against Barrenness: *For Success in Business and Life*

Fruit of the Womb: *Prayers Against Barrenness*

Beauty Curses, *Warfare Prayers Against*
https://a.co/d/5Xlc20M

Courts of Marriage: Prayers for Marriage in the Courts of Heaven *(prayerbook)*
https://a.co/d/cNAdgAq

Courtroom Warfare @ Midnight
(prayerbook) https://a.co/d/5fc7Qdp

Demonic Cobwebs *(prayerbook)*
https://a.co/d/fp9Oa2H

Every Evil Bird https://a.co/d/hF1kh1O

Gates of Thanksgiving

I AM NOT YOUR TARGET: *Warfare Against Haters & the Powers They Employ*

Spirits of Death, Hell & the Grave, Pass Over Me and My House

Throne of Grace: Courtroom Prayer

Warfare Prayer Against Poverty
https://a.co/d/bZ61lYu

Other books by this author

AK: The Adventures of the Agape Kid

Already Married in the Spirit: *Why You May Not Be Married in the Natural*

AMONG SOME THIEVES
https://a.co/d/dkYT4ZV

Ancestral Powers

Anti-Marriage, *The Spirit of*

Backstabbers https://a.co/d/gi8iBxf

Barrenness, *Prayers Against* https://a.co/d/feUltIs

Battlefield of Marriage, *The*

Beware of the Dog: Prayers Against Dogs in the Dream.

Bless Your Food: *Let the Dining Table be Undefiled*

Blindsided: *Has the Old Man Bewitched You?* https://a.co/d/5O2fLLR

Break Free from Collective Captivity

Broken Spirits & Dry Bones

By Means of a Whorish Father

Casting Down Imaginations

Churchzilla, The Wanna-Be, Supposed-to-be Bride of Christ

Demonic Cobwebs (prayerbook)

Demonic Time Bombs

Demons Hate Questions

Devil Loves Trauma, *The*

Devil Weapons: Unforgiveness, Bitterness,...

The Devourers: Thieves of Darkness 2

Discernment: The Unabridged Guide

Do Not Swear by the Moon

Don't Refuse Me, Lord (4 book series) https://a.co/d/idP34LG

Dream Defilement

The Emptiers: *Thieves of Darkness, 1* https://a.co/d/5I4n5mc

Evil Touch

Failed Assignment

Fantasy Spirit Spouse https://a.co/d/hW7oYbX

FAT Demons (The): *Breaking Demonic Curses* https://a.co/d/4kP8wV1

The Fold (5-book series)

- The Fold (Book 1)
- Name Your Seed (Book 2)
- The Poor Attitudes of Money (3)
- Do Not Orphan Your Seed (4)
- For the Sake of the Gospel (5)
- My Sowing Journal

Gang Ups: Touch Not God's Anointed

Getting Rid of Evil Spiritual Food

https://a.co/d/i2L3WYQ

got HEALING? Verses for Life

got LOVE? Verses for Life

got HOPE? Verses for Life

got money?   https://a.co/d/g2av41N

Here Come the Horns: *Skilled to Destroy*
https://a.co/d/cZiNnkP

Hidden Sins: Hidden Iniquity

https://a.co/d/4Mth0wa

How to Dental Assist

How to Dental Assist2: Be Productive, Not Wasteful

How to STOP Being a Blind Witch or Warlock

I AM NOT YOUR TARGET: *Warfare Against Haters and the Powers they Employ*

I Take It Back

Keepsakes or Mistakes

Legacy

Let Me Have A Dollar's Worth
https://a.co/d/h8F8XgE

Level the Playing Field

Living for the NOW of God

Lose My Location
https://a.co/d/crD6mV9

Love Breaks Your Heart

Made Perfect In Love

Mammon https://a.co/d/29yhMG7

Man Safari, *The*

Marriage Ed. Rules of Engagement & Marriage

Made Perfect in Love

Money Hunters: Beware of Those

Money on the Altar https://a.co/d/4EqJ2Nr

Mulberry Tree, *The*
https://a.co/d/9nR9rRb

Motherboard (The) - *Soul Prosperity Series*

Name Your Seed

Occupy: *Until I Return*
https://a.co/d/bZ7ztUy

Plantation Souls

Players Gonna Play

Portals: Shut the Front Door: Prayers to Close Evil Portals.

Power Money: Nine Times the Tithe

https://a.co/d/gRt41gy

The Power to Get Wealth
https://a.co/d/e4ub4Ov

Powers Above

The Robe, Part 1, The Lessons of Joseph

The Robe, Part II, The Lessons of Joseph

Seasons of Grief

Seasons of Waiting

Seasons of War

Second Marriage, Third--, *Any Marriage*
https://a.co/d/6m6GN4N

Seducing Spirits: Idolatry & Whoredoms
https://a.co/d/4Jq4WEs

Shut the Front Door: *Prayers to Close Portals* https://a.co/d/cH4TWJj

Sift You Like Wheat

Six Men Short: What Has Happened to all the Men?

SLAVE

Soul Prosperity soul prosperity series 3

https://a.co/d/5p8YvCN

Souls Captivity soul prosperity series 2

The Spirit of Anti-Marriage

The Spirit of Poverty
https://a.co/d/abV2o2e

Spiritual Thieves https://a.co/d/eqPPz33

StarStruck- Triangular Power series.

SUNBLOCK- Triangular Power series.

The Swallowers: *Thieves of Darkness*, 3

Take It Back

This Is NOT That: How to Keep Demons from Coming at You

Time Is of the Essence

Too Many Wives: *Why You Have Lady Problems*

Tormenting Spirits
https://a.co/d/dAogEJf

Toxic Souls

Triangular Power *(series)*

- Powers Above
- SUNBLOCK
- Do Not Swear by the Moon
- STARSTRUCK

Unbreak My Heart: *Don't Let Me Die*

Uncontested Doom

Unguarded Hours, *The*

Unseen Life, *The* (forthcoming)

Upgrade: How to Get Out of Survival Mode

- Toxic Souls (Book 2 of series)
- Legacy (Book 3 of series)

The Wasters: *Thieves of Darkness,* Bk 2
https://a.co/d/bUvI9Jo

What Have You to Declare? What Do You Have With You from Where You've Been?

When I Was A Child, *I Prayed As a Child*

When the Devourer is Rebuked

https://a.co/d/1HVv8oq

The Wilderness Romance *(series)* This series is about conducting a Godly relationship and marriage with someone who is a Wilderness person. It is about how to recognize it and navigate through it. These books are about how not to get caught up in such.

- *The Social Wilderness*
- *The Sexual Wilderness*
- *The Spiritual Wilderness*

Other Series

The Fold (a series on Godly finances)
https://a.co/d/4hz3unj

Soul Prosperity Series https://a.co/d/bz2M42q

Spirit Spouse books

https://a.co/d/9VehDSo

https://a.co/d/97sKOwm

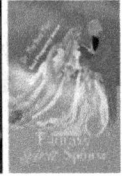

Battlefield of Marriage, The

https://a.co/d/eUDzizO

Players Gonna Play

https://a.co/d/2hzGw3N

Sent Spirit Spouse (can someone send you a spirit spouse? This book is not yet released.)

Matters of the Heart

Made Perfect in Love
https://a.co/d/70MQW3O

Love Breaks Your Heart
https://a.co/d/4KvuQLZ

Unbreak My Heart
https://a.co/d/84ceZ6M

Broken Spirits & Dry Bones
https://a.co/d/e6iedNP

Thieves of Darkness series

The Emptiers https://a.co/d/heio0dO

The Wasters https://a.co/d/5TG1iNQ

The Swallowers https://a.co/d/1jWhM6G

The Devourers: Why We Can't Have Nice Things https://a.co/d/87Tejbf

Spiritual Thieves

Triangular Powers https://a.co/d/aUCjAWC

Upgrade (series) *How to Get Out of Survival Mode* https://a.co/d/aTERhX0

www.ingramcontent.com/pod-product-compliance
Lightning Source LLC
Chambersburg PA
CBHW070456100426
42743CB00010B/1644